I looked at my gun, sitting on the table. "There's nothing left; why not?"

I picked up the gun and put a magazine in it. I cocked it, opened my mouth, stuck the gun down my throat and pulled the trigger.

Click!

No explosion! Nothing but a click! I took the bullet out. There was an indentation on the shell where the hammer had struck it. Yet it hadn't fired! I cursed it and loaded the pistol again.

I opened my mouth and pulled the trigger.

Click!

I slammed the gun against the wall, then looked up at the ceiling and cursed God! "I hate you, God! You won't even let me die! I don't understand what you want of me! Just let me die!" Then I gathered up some more pills and washed them down with the rest of my liquor . . .

"What," I thought, "does God want of me? . . . I can't stand to live, and He won't let me die! Why is He picking on me?"

Chosen to Live

David F. Kelton

with R. Russell Bixler

Foreword by Demos Shakarian

CHOSEN TO LIVE

Art Work by Waltraud Hendel
Layout by Helen Mierski
Typesetting by Jean Stewart

Contents

Foreword by Demos Shakarian 5

1. Atheists and Arguments 7
2. My World Collapses 19
3. Dropping Out 35
4. Always Lucky! 45
5. Brinda 53
6. Journey to Disaster 63
7. Can a Dead Man Work a Miracle? 75
8. "I Hate Miracles!" 89
9. One of Us Had to Die 103
10. Opening Doors 119
11. Television 129
12. New Frontiers 143
13. Learning to Expect the Impossible 155

Epilogue: The Healings Continue 165

Foreword

One of the greatest acts of grace I have ever seen transpired in the life of David Kelton.

David came into my life unexpectedly one day in 1970 at a Full Gospel Business Men's meeting in Charlotte, North Carolina. That meeting changed his life — and mine! If I ever had any doubts that God works miracles today, I need only think of David. As he related the story to me — how he was an atheist when he attended our Full Gospel Businessmen's meeting, and the miraculous physical healing he received that evening — I was shocked! Here was a man who didn't even believe in God, and yet God healed him!

I went to my Bible to search what the Scriptures had to say and found that Jesus did indeed heal the sick — and then told them to go and sin no more. David Kelton experienced this personally, and today is one of God's choice vessels and one of His great soul winners.

I recommend this book to everyone. It will inspire you and give you hope.

Demos Shakarian
International President
Full Gospel Business Men's Fellowship

Chapter 1

Atheists and Arguments

No one saw the wreck, but a North Carolina state trooper heard the collision a mile down the highway. When he arrived at the scene minutes later, the patrolman fainted!

Even in the midnight darkness he could see hands and arms scattered throughout the wreckage, which was strewn over hundreds of yards. Five people died instantly in that collision, caused by two drunken drivers, smashing head-on at an approach speed of at least 150 miles per hour. The crash was so terrible that both cars were welded together. Mike was driving his big Ford sedan and I was lying on the back seat, in a drunken stupor from a combination of wine and pills.

Even the impact of the crash did not arouse me, although my jaw was shattered and ripped loose from the skull. My neck was broken, the roof of my mouth was split in two, my left eye was dislodged from its socket, and I sustained massive internal injuries. My left leg was crushed beneath the engine and transmission, which had come to rest where the rear window had been. After the trooper recovered from his shock, he set out flares along the highway. While walking back to the wreckage, he heard a groan. Reaching inside, he shined his flashlight on me — and passed out again!

No one could believe I was alive, yet there I was — still breathing, with blood all over me. Gasoline covered everything, but the imminent fire never occurred. The medical people held out little hope for my survival, but if they could amputate my left leg, they could at least get the rest of me from under the engine and into the hospital. A man who lived nearby was called from his bed and promptly arrived with his newly-invented machine, an apparatus designed to pull wrecked cars apart in order to rescue people trapped inside. At the very moment he completed ripping the cars apart with his invention, the ambulance arrived with the doctor who intended to amputate my left leg. I was taken to the hospital — still unconscious — but all in one piece. It was as if I had been *chosen* to live!

This story is very difficult to tell. Only the urging of my wife and everyone else close to me could lead me to share the things you will read. You will understand my reluctance.

My father was an atheist. He got it naturally: Dad's father and grandfather had been atheists, also. Mom was raised by Christian parents, but two of her aunts were spiritualist mediums. They had tried to interest my mother in their occult practices, but even as a little girl, Mom knew it was wrong. She would have none of it.

We children were in trouble before we came into this world. My older sister Marquita was born without eyes; I almost died soon after birth; my younger brother Tim was born a hemophiliac; and Nathan, the baby of the family, was near death many times as the result of severe asthma attacks.

I was born near Kansas City during a severe snowstorm in 1941. Mom was a Pentecostal, so she invited two friends from the church to pray with her during the delivery. The doctor fought his way through the blizzard to our house, but Mom suffered in labor for many hours. The storm kept the doctor at our home, so he ate and slept there. Mom's two faithful prayer-partners prayed with her that whole time, and when I was finally born, each woman was holding one of her hands and praying in tongues earnestly. Mom was praying in tongues right along with them.

Mom knew I'd be all right, even though I was

near death. She'd already learned what God can do. Five years earlier she and Dad were anticipating the birth of their first child, when Mom had an ominous dream: she saw her little baby girl with no eyes. And that's exactly what occurred — Marquita was born without eyeballs.

The reactions to this tragedy by Mom and Dad were quite different. Dad was heartbroken. Although we were poor, Dad told the finest ophthalmologist in the state that he would do anything if only his daughter could see. After an examination, the doctor, with tears in his eyes, told my father not to waste his money. "No specialist can do anything: she has no eyeballs."

Mom spent the first days after Marquita's birth in repentance. She felt guilty for having married an atheist, so she was spending much time asking God to forgive her. In fact, as a teenager she had felt that she should be a foreign missionary, but had disobeyed God after falling in love with Dad. Mom continued to pray tearfully for her newly-born Marquita, until an incident occurred while she was reading the Gospel of John. Jesus' disciples were asking if a certain man had been born blind because of his own sin or his parents' sin. "Jesus answered, 'Neither hath this man sinned, nor his parents: but that the works of God should be made manifest in him.'" The words of that verse appeared to leap off the page, seeming to

Mom's eyes to stand up in a three-dimensional effect. She began to cry with joy and to praise God.

Each day thereafter, as Mom gently washed away the sticky substance that oozed out of Marquita's empty sockets, she would look eagerly for new eyes. Her sisters and neighbors thought the grief had left her deranged, for she repeatedly told them that God was going to create eyes for Marquita. One day, as she was bathing her seven-week-old baby's eyelids, she noticed the first tear. Excitement exploded in Mom's heart. Marquita's eyelids began to flutter, and then they opened to reveal two beautiful brown eyes! Mom erupted in shouts of praise!

Snatching Marquita into her arms, she ran out on the porch, screaming to anyone who could hear: "Come look at my miracle baby! God gave her new eyes!" Neighbors flocked from all directions! My grandfather was working in his garden a block away, but he heard the screaming and came running, too. Hurrying to the dairy, Grandpa told Dad to come home quickly. When he saw Marquita, Dad fell on the bed, sobbing. He promptly made the grateful commitment he mistakenly thought God would desire of him: Dad gave up smoking — permanently!

Without even examining the baby, the ophthalmologist began to cry the moment he saw

Marquita. He knew that a miracle had taken place. The doctor, admitting that he had once been a Christian, rededicated his life to God on the spot — and died of a heart attack several weeks later!

After almost fifty years, Marquita's eyesight remains excellent today! Her miraculous story has affected countless people.

Dad and Mom argued about things that we children didn't understand. Both of them were strong-willed. Mom thought the devil resided in a deck of cards, but Dad saw nothing wrong with it. In fact, Dad was a compulsive gambler. Mom wouldn't even allow us to use the dice that were a part of our Monopoly game — we had to use a spinning arrow! It seemed to me as a child that Dad was always arguing in favor of good things; Mom (and God) stood resolutely opposed to all that was enjoyable. Certain that all of heaven was on her side, Mom would not budge, and inevitably Dad would give in. After all, he couldn't forget what God had done for his baby in response to Mom's prayers.

Dad despised the Pentecostal church Mom wanted to attend, and vowed that he would never drive her there. Stubbornly Mom walked the two miles every Sunday morning. Sunday after Sunday we had to walk to church with Mom, rain or shine. Occasionally Dad would pass us in the car as we silently trudged those two miles, but he would never do one thing to help us go to church. Surely Dad was driving somewhere exciting, but we kids have got to be miserable — for God! Mom's relationship with the Lord was real and precious, and she assumed that everyone else should have so wonderful a relationship. One woman in that church was literally a "holy roller," and she would create awful scenes every Sunday! Even as a little child I became thoroughly disgusted with the hypocrisy that was so evident. What kind of a Person is this God, anyway?

Grandpa — Mom's father — and my Dad "hit it off" quite well. During the Great Depression, the two families had survived by living and working together for a period. Dad was tall, strong and handsome, while my grandfather was short and stocky, with strong arms — he could whip almost anybody in arm wrestling. Grandpa had a quick temper, too. Sometimes he would give no warning, but just explode into action. I realized more and more as I was growing up that I was like my grandfather. I think he realized it, too.

Mom said I was a model child. Even from an early age, I kept my clothes and toys neat. I even waxed the floor of my own bedroom!

Dad would hold me on his lap and read children's books to me, and he enjoyed watching me memorize the words and read the books back to him. One day, when I was four years old, he noticed that I was reading a "grown-up" book out loud. He questioned Mom, asking if she had read it to me earlier. Quickly they realized that I had actually taught myself to read at the age of four! Tears filled Dad's eyes. He picked me up and told me how great I was going to be.

Dad began seeing in me the success he should have been, instead of the failure he thought he was. His father had been a superintendent on the Frisco Railroad, and his grandfather had been a medical doctor who owned a great deal of property in Arkansas. I didn't understand what Dad was talking about as he praised my abilities, but I sure knew he loved me. He encouraged me in a number of areas, perceiving that I was a most gifted youngster.

When I was five years old, Marquita became ill with the measles, and I would sit in her bedroom reading my children's books to her every day. It wasn't long before I was tutoring Marquita in mathematics, although she was five years older.

After I entered school, the principal encouraged me to proceed with my studies as rapidly as I wished. Because I enjoyed learning, I loved school. I had natural leadership ability, earned the highest grades, and was one of the elementary school's best athletes. Dad was a good baseball player, and he was so proud when I made the Little League all-star team several consecutive years. I even learned to play the violin, becoming so proficient that later I almost made first chair in the high school orchestra.

Just before my ninth birthday Dad and Mom gave me a Christmas gift that was to change my life — a ouija board. Never realizing the satanic nature of this deceptive little game, she who was always afraid "the devil would get" me, was herself taken in by the devil, and I paid the penalty for it. Mom would pray all the time Dad and I were watching television — "the devil's box" — yet she didn't grasp the more serious occult problem in the ouija board. Utterly fascinated by that ouija board, I was soon reading every occult book I could find in the North Kansas City public library. I wanted eagerly to be able to control other people. The seeds of my future problems had been sown.

I found I liked girls, too. When I was twelve years old, I was interested in a most-sexually-active girl of eleven who encouraged petting. One evening I was helping her undress in the basement of her home when her father suddenly walked downstairs. He rebuked his daughter severely and went upstairs to telephone my father. Dad came to

15

get me, gently giving me my first lesson in the facts of life. He warned me that sexual activity would lead to pregnancy, which would require that we get married, and you shouldn't get so involved with a girl because you might not love her, and you only want to marry the girl you love. I got the message.

But Mom! Mom exploded with religious indignation! She just knew the devil was going to get me unless I straightened out. Surely Dad must have wished he hadn't told her about the incident.

It was about this time that Dad finally made a "religious" commitment. Actually, he never seemed to understand what Christianity was all about, although he sincerely tried. He even began attending church with us. Dad was what our culture would call a "good" man, friendly and outgoing, but apparently burdened with a sense of failure and guilt. He seemed to equate Christianity with a set of negative rules, and his addiction to gambling kept his conscience rubbed raw.

One earlier Christmas eve Dad had come home drunk with a brand-new washing machine for Mom. He was so happy to present her with the very gift she wanted so badly.

"Where did you get the money for that washer?" she demanded. "You won that money gambing, didn't you?"

"Well, . . . yeah, I guess."

"You take that washer right back where you got it! I won't have the devil's money buying me a washing machine!"

"Aw, Myda . . ."

"You get that machine out of here!" The argument went on and on, but the result was foregone. I watched the scene with genuine grief as Dad reluctantly returned the washer.

Every time my Dad wanted to do something nice, it was always "God" who was opposed to it. One day he took us kids to a "picture show." Mom had a fit! I loved the movie, but obviously God hated it. So Dad's sense of guilt deepened, although he made a commitment to God as best as he could understand.

There were so many things that Mom considered evil. She lectured us repeatedly about the evils of drinking coffee. Mom wouldn't even allow us to go swimming or attend a school square dance. I was greatly embarrassed when my seventh grade teacher mockingly read to the whole class Mom's letter explaining the evils of dancing. To this day I still can't swim, and I still can't dance.

Chapter 2

My World Collapses

In 1955 I graduated from the eighth grade and entered high school. As one of more than twelve hundred students, I was no longer the model student, the leader, no longer the smartest, no longer the best athlete. I was overwhelmed! As a result of the accelerated program in elementary school, I had already read many of what would ultimately be my high school textbooks. I had even done some college-level math. The high school classes were structured, repetitive and quite boring. I made the freshmen football team, but not first-string, apparently being considered too small. This was such a shock after being one of the best athletes in our little elementary school.

One terrible afternoon a minister came to get me at football practice. With a heavy heart he told me that my six-foot, two-inch, forty-one-year-old, healthy, strong father had just died of a heart attack!

Words could not describe my feelings. I was

totally devastated! I was told that God had taken my father. Not God! — again?

"Now you're the man of the family" became such a despised statement. How could God be so cruel as to take my father? I couldn't support a mother and two younger brothers: I was only fourteen!

We had always been poor; now we became poorer as Mom found the only job she was trained for — in a school cafeteria.

Normally figuring things out for myself, I pondered more than ever this business about God. After perhaps a year of thinking about the matter, I decided there was no God! God was mere superstition. So there! That solved a lot of seeming inconsistencies for me. But what about my sister's eyes? I decided that Mom and Dad had been lying about Marquita's miracle. Quickly learning the technique of the atheist, I practiced closing my eyes to any facts that violated my atheism.

I decided further that no one would ever again hurt me. I would never love anybody, including my own family. I would dominate other people for my own benefit: no one would ever dominate me. That was quite a series of decisions for a fifteen-year-old!

Seething with resentment, I quit football

and baseball, and took up boxing — anything to express my hostility. Bored with the tedium of high school material I had long since learned, I became a trouble-maker in class. Repeatedly I was reprimanded and embarrassed by teachers for having read high school textbooks during elementary school. My geometry teacher the following year told me he'd give me a "B" if I would stay out of class the rest of the year. "You already know the material," he explained. Thus he got rid of a serious problem — me!

I felt a restlessness that was new to me. I'd lie down to go to sleep, but soon I was back on my feet, looking for something to occupy my mind. A deep anxiety seemed to take up residence within me.

The first summer after Dad died, I got a job racking balls in a pool hall. After learning to shoot pool, I improved so much that I was soon winning money from grown men. I began running around with a different type of boys. In order to finance our beer and cigarettes, we began to steal from a local bakery. We learned how to break into a soft-drink warehouse and steal cases of empty soft drink bottles, which we would turn in at various stores for the deposit. Soon we had successfully stolen and sold hundreds of cases of empty bottles.

One night we took the back seat out of a boy's

car and were loading it with bottles. I was wheeling out a handtruck full of cases when a police car came around the corner. I ran for a cornfield and kept running, in spite of the cop's warning. When shotgun pellets started hitting cornstalks, I decided it was time to stop running. After being taken to jail, I learned the value of a bold lie when we told them we had never stolen before. The soft drink company believed us and refused to press charges. We were released. In one night I had three educational experiences: I was shot at for the first time, I spent my first hours in a jail cell, and I learned how to lie to the police convincingly.

After calling my grandfather, the police led him and Mom into the jail. The three of us walked to the car in silence, and rode home in silence; almost nothing was said. Mom understood the evils of picture shows and television, but my escapades into drinking and stealing were beyond her ability to cope.

My friends and I obtained gasoline by siphoning it out of trucks. We also stole hubcaps for resale. One night a policeman caught us with a car full of stolen hubcaps. We thought we were in serious trouble until he made us put them in the trunk of his squad car, and then let us go. Again my education was expanded: I lost all respect for cops.

Most of my school time was spent in the pool hall. The teachers didn't want me in class, anyway. The principal's office didn't find out I was skipping school because a couple of girls who liked me had access to the attendance records.

Mom had always prayed earnestly for us, but she was in such a state of shock for the first couple of years after Dad's death. Overwhelmed with grief, fully occupied with earning a meager living, and caring for my younger brothers was more than she could handle. Now I was sixteen, and still I resisted any feeling of responsibility for my family. Mom told me I wasn't allowed to work in the pool hall, but I calmly defied her and walked out the door.

The following summer a friend and I decided we didn't like Kansas City, so we left for California. I said nothing to Mom, but wrote a note saying only that I was leaving home. A man picked us up in Oklahoma and dropped us off in Modesto. We nearly froze, trying to sleep in the orange groves. Wandering over California, we gravitated to various hippie groups. I was fascinated by the allure of hordes of sophisticated youngsters who hated God, hated their parents, hated the government, and exalted Marxism and the occult. They seemed to have unlimited money, drugs, beer and sex. I plunged in — *almost* all the way. Somehow in high school I had been frightened half-to-death by a lecture on venereal disease; between that and Dad's quiet lesson about sex, I always stopped short of sexual intercourse, although illicit sex was a prominent aspect of the drop-out culture there. I was awed by the whole California hippie life style. Without money however, we quickly "wore out our welcome," so we had no choice but to return home after a month.

Mom never gave up on me. As God's healing power began comforting and strengthening her, she started praying more earnestly for me. She was already experiencing some dramatic miracles of material provision in the midst of poverty. Mom enjoyed an ever-deepening trust in God's goodness and care. But her talk about the Lord only infuriated me. Marquita had gotten married just before Dad died, and Mom struggled courageously to support Tim and Nathan, who were seven and nine years younger than I. They were always good boys, and they simply couldn't understand me.

I was even different from the boys and girls I ran around with. They would be content with two or three cans of beer, but my restlessness drove me to keep on drinking. They enjoyed each other, but I enjoyed getting drunk and staying drunk. I was developing quite a reputation as a teenage drinker. The other kids drank because they didn't feel loved at home, but I knew Mom loved me, and before his death Dad had loved me too. Grandpa always seemed to love me no matter what I had done. My life wasn't lacking in love; I simply was filled with anxiety. And I was bitter over events — a happy childhood suddenly turned sour by high school boredom and disappointment and by my father's untimely death. So I drank and drank to escape it all.

When we returned from California, the high school refused to accept me for my junior year because I had caused so much trouble the year before. My aunt and uncle across town allowed me to live with them and go to a different high school. They were going to make me a good boy. My uncle found a part-time job for me in a grocery store, where my most notable accomplishment was stealing beer. Soon realizing that I was incorrigible, my uncle sent me back to live with Mom and my brothers.

The following summer I found a job in a machine shop. The owner was quite well-to-do, and he was so struck by my ability to learn and apply mechanical skills that he wanted to adopt me. He actually wanted to give his whole business to me some day. But Mom wasn't interested in the least — I was *her boy*! She wouldn't even discuss the matter.

My senior year consisted of taking a couple of

hours of classes each day and spending the rest of my time shooting pool, gambling, drinking and fighting. I loved to fight, and I was pretty good at it. Not really caring whether I lived or died, I was sick of the whole world!

On impulse I dropped out of school just three weeks before I was to graduate. Already forming the pattern of walking out before completing anything, I had quit football, I had quit orchestra, I had quit church and God, I had quit a number of my classes, I had even quit my family.

Continuing to drink and fight, I was usually careful not to commit those "sins" Dad and Mom had specifically warned me about when I was a child. For example, I didn't touch coffee until years later. I would engage in petting with the girls, but I was still quite inhibited by my father's warning about sexual intercourse. About this time even that restraint broke down, and I began having an affair with a rather pleasant, friendly girl named Judy. Each time I was with Judy I enjoyed myself, but the next day would experience a sense of guilt. I didn't feel any love for Judy, so we broke up.

The thrill of California was always in the back of my mind, so I headed west to enjoy another fling, hopefully to stay there. I left Kansas City during the closing days of July with San Francisco as my goal. The allure of the outwardly-happy hippie culture drew me. All of that marijuana, alcohol, drugs, money and sex was hypnotic. I loved the hippie message of atheism and Marxism; I too wanted to be a part of overthrowing the government. That goal helped me to focus my bitterness.

But I couldn't find a job in California, so a few weeks later I returned to Kansas City. Within hours after arriving home, I received a telephone call from Judy, who asked me to come to see her. All my excitement about California and sex and atheism and Marxism was dashed on the rocks of reality when Judy told me she was pregnant. The memory of Dad's gentle lecture came roaring into my conscious mind: "If you ever get a girl pregnant, you'll have to marry her, and you might not be in love." Dad's word's were prophetic.

Judy's mother was a Christian, and she felt we shouldn't get married since we didn't love each other. I was adamant: my Dad had said we would have to get married! So we did, in September of 1959. Mom tried to warn me: "Are you sure it's your baby?" But Mom didn't know much about the real world, I thought, and I ignored her. Cindy was born the following May.

Judy, who was sixteen when we married, dropped out of school and found a job. Her pregnancy sobered me for a time, but, try as I would, I simply could not find work in Kansas City. I enrolled in the Electronics Institute, partially paid for by my Dad's Social Security benefits. Immediately my talents were noted, and the school made me a lab instructor. Before long they were using me to help teach a course.

Then I heard that Armco Steel in California was hiring, so I drove west again. They gave me a job, and Judy and little Cindy followed on the train. Very quickly the union shop steward at Armco told me I was working too fast, although I was hardly exerting myself. So the union saw to it that I lost my incentive pay. This only hardened my belief that the whole world was rotten.

A few months later I was laid off, so Judy and I returned to Kansas City. All through this period I had affairs with other girls. When Judy confronted me, I admitted it freely. I had been trained as a boy to tell the truth, and I seldom lied (except to the police). My usual attitude, whenever I was caught doing anything wrong, was, "That's right! What are you going to do about it?" Most of the time my bold defiance was so shocking that I would get away with it.

One time another fellow and I were in a large variety store. Just for the thrill of it, we filled a goldfish bowl full of water from an aquarium, threw a bunch of goldfish in it, and started out the door. I was holding the bowl with two hands when the security guard asked to see our receipt. I laughed, "You don't think we'd try to steal a bowl of goldfish, do you?" He laughed too — and let us go without showing the receipt. I probably wouldn't have cared if I had been caught; I hated myself. We sold the goldfish for enough to buy a few drinks.

Judy tried to make our marriage work, but I would walk out and live with another girl for several days, or come home drunk, or gamble away Judy's money. Finally, we agreed to call it off permanently, and I saw little Cindy only twice after our separation. Later, Judy married a man much nicer than I, and he provided a stable home for Cindy. Walking out on my wife and baby seemed to pile an intolerable load of guilt on me, and I began to work more earnestly at destroying myself.

After I left Judy, Mom remodeled a room for me over the garage, and another girl moved in there with me. Most of the time I was stoned on drugs or booze, financing myself with petty crimes and burglaries. It seemed that the more Mom prayed for me, the more depraved and miserable I got.

My cousin Terry Sue, a very pretty girl almost my age, also prayed earnestly for me for years. Although my brother Tim was seven years younger, he seemed to have been born with a pastor's heart, and he prayed and tried even as a boy to help me. But Mom! She spent hours on her knees, interceding on my behalf. Soon God began to honor her prayers in some unusual ways.

One day about seven or eight fellows from across the river came to the isolated roadhouse where I often hung out. They had heard about my reputation at shooting pool, so they brought their local expert. I discovered very quickly that he wasn't as good as he thought he was. Two of my friends were betting on me, and between us we took them for about nine hundred dollars. Some angry words led to pushing and threatening, and the fight spilled out into the back alley. At that moment Mom was eating at her sister's home, when suddenly she jumped up from the table: "David's in trouble!"

"David's always in trouble," intoned her brother-in-law.

"I have to go!"

"Oh Myda!" complained my aunt. "At least finish your dinner. How do you know David's in trouble?"

Mom didn't argue further. She dashed out the door and ran to her car. She drove the fifteen miles as fast as she could — right to the very alley where I was indeed in trouble. Seeing one of these guys with a big hunting knife at my back, Mom boldly stopped her car beside us, leaned over, opened the opposite door and shouted sternly, "David! Get in the car!" Those seven or eight men meekly let me get in the car, and we drove off.

"David, God showed me that you were in trouble."

"Aw, Mom! Don't give me that 'God' stuff again."

"He did, David! He loves you. That's why He saved you from those hoodlums."

I just sulked, I knew there wasn't any God. Yet, how did she find me in that alley at that very moment? How did she know? Christians, I decided, are opportunists. They give God credit for every good coincidence. "I prayed!" they exult. Or, "It's a miracle! Praise the Lord!" A Christian calls every coincidence a miracle, thus I reasoned. "That's how Mom is trying to prove that God exists." I had it all figured out. "If it were really true, Dad would not have died." I got so sick of Mom's praising God for everything! "She's just ignorant," I told myself, "afraid to face the real world."

I faced my own problem — the continual need for money. I couldn't hold a job long, so I was

31

always open to any idea for obtaining cash quickly. One of my friends whose father was a sheep farmer suggested that we could rustle one of his sheep and sell it at the stockyards in Leavenworth, Kansas. His father wouldn't miss one sheep. So he took the back seat out of his car, and we headed for the farm. It had just been raining, and we tried to catch a sheep in the darkness. We slipped and fell in the mud, the sheep squirmed out of our grasp repeatedly, the back of his car was all mud when we finally got the sheep in there, and we were both totally exhausted. The next morning, when we took it to Leavenworth and tried to sell it, the man looked at the sheep's ear and carefully noted the brand. He called the police and the boy's father. The cops loved it. "Boys! You're in Kansas now! Here in this state we used to hang rustlers. That hanging law is still on the books!" Of course, the police knew that my friend's father wouldn't press charges, so they tried to frighten us. They succeeded, too. We were terrified! It was my first and last attempt at rustling.

One day a couple of us decided to drive to St. Louis, where nobody knew me, so we could hustle some money shooting pool. Two fifteen-year-old girls who wanted to run away from home heard us talking about it and asked to go along. Somehow their parents discovered that the girls were with us, and they called the State Police.

We were picked up and taken to a small-town jail where the girls taunted the drunken jailer with filthy, suggestive language and sexual advances. He got so angry that he and his assistant came downstairs to our cell, handcuffed us to the bars and beat us mercilessly with "beanbags" — lead pellets in leather pouches. "You big-city punks have got to learn to stay in Kansas City!" he panted between swings. Beanbags are designed to hurt badly while they leave no obvious bruises.

The next day a man claiming to be with the F.B.I. came to our cell and told us how many years in jail we could get for statutory rape (since the girls were under sixteen). The girls, however, lied and signed affidavits that we hadn't touched them. The moment we were released, we headed back for Kansas City as fast as we could go.

Chapter Three

Dropping Out

My uncle was the principal of a Christian school in Charlotte, and he offered Mom a job in the school cafeteria. She accepted and moved to North Carolina with Tim and Nathan, leaving me alone in that room over the garage. That was the most miserable winter I have ever experienced. Not doing a bit of honest work for a year, I was stoned all the time, supporting myself with petty crime — snatching purses, stealing hubcaps, gambling at pool, always taking pills and drinking booze. I walked the streets of Kansas City in the snow with holes in my shoes, thinking that nobody cared about me.

Suddenly Mom arrived from Charlotte. "David, come to Charlotte with us. You can get a new start there."

I wasn't interested. I was drunk when she found me, so Mom agreed to drive me to one of the bars where I hung out. But I passed out in her car, and Mom turned for North Carolina instead. We were halfway there before I woke up. I became very angry, and she could keep me in the car only by promising to send me back to Kansas City on the bus after a brief visit.

After I got to Charlotte, my uncle talked with me about my abilities. He told me that he might be able to get me into college if I would do well on their exams, even though I didn't have a high school diploma. He explained personally to the Chancellor of the University of North Carolina at Charlotte that I really hadn't had a chance because of my father's death. It was agreed that, if I made a certain score on the high school equivalency test and several hundred points *above* the normal minimum on the college entrance examination, only then would I be allowed to enroll as a college freshman. Both my uncle and the Chancellor were staggered by the scores I made. They were genuinely excited about me. This seemed to the Chancellor to be a humanitarian act, an opportunity to redeem a gifted student from a wasted life. They felt I should major in electronics engineering.

Suddenly I had an intellectual challenge again — the first since the eighth grade. I studied hard and earned high grades during the first semester. However, I also became acquainted with

36

the drinking students and started skipping classes.

A Jewish girl and I really found a lot in common. We both liked to drink, we hated the rest of the world, and we were attracted to Marxism. She joked about taking me to meet her father and telling him that we were engaged — just to hurt him — "that rich, capitalistic father of mine!" Sex was involved in our relationship, but it was secondary to our mutual love of drinking.

One morning I was walking to take my final exams at the end of the freshman year, when I met this Jewish girl. "Do you want to get a bottle?" I asked.

"Let's go!" she responded.

We bought two fifths of vodka and got drunk out in the parking lot. I never went back to the University. After completing almost a full year, I quit again!

Gravitating to the poolrooms of Charlotte, I gambled and won consistently — until I would get so worn out from continual drugs that any good pool player could beat me. "Stick with him!" coached the wiser heads when my opponent was losing to me. A few hours later he was taking his money back as I began to lose my concentration.

With no warning I received my greetings from

Uncle Sam. I was drafted, and Vietnam would be my destination.

Being a confirmed Marxist, I was strongly anti-war and anti-establishment. Yet, for some strange reason, I felt I should accept conscription into the Army.

All through my life I would do everything correctly for a period, then I would reverse my behavior and do everything wrong. As difficult as it was, I cooperated fully in my nine weeks of basic training. When basic training was completed, I was given the "Outstanding Trainee" award at a special ceremony. Mom received a letter from the colonel, telling her that I was "an outstanding example of American youth." Today that may sound humorous, but I didn't think so. I always felt I was better than other people, anyhow, especially after I'd wake up from a drunken stupor. People wondered why I would do so well at the beginning of a project or job or school curriculum, only to fail later. It was because of that very arrogant attitude: I wanted to prove to everybody that I did not *have* to be a common drunk — I was a drunk because I *chose* to be a drunk!

The "Outstanding Trainee" award made Mom so proud of me. It gave her hope, and she kept right on praying for her wayward son. I received several more commendations during that first year in the Army. Becoming an expert marksman, I developed a lifelong love of guns. As usual, however, I began to drink heavily again. I just couldn't seem to drink in moderation for an extended period. That driving anxiety within me refused to be suppressed.

Then I discovered the codeine in cough syrup. At that time it was available in large quantities at cheap prices. I would plan how many drinks and how much cough syrup I could buy with my next pay. Since my money was limited, I began to frequent the black sections of town near the Army base in Louisiana; prices were cheaper there. Soon I was able to finance all the drinks and drugs I wanted with the money I won shooting pool.

It wasn't long before I was receiving disciplinary action for missing curfew or making 5:30 a.m. roll call dead drunk. As I had been awarded commendations the first year, so I was repeatedly disciplined my second year in the Army. Punishment, however, was always limited because of my record of commendations. Receiving many lectures by those in authority over me, I endured them in silent arrogance, because I knew I was superior to the whole United States Army.

The alcohol and drugs were leading to the reassertion of the Marxism and anti-establishment profanity coming from my lips. Finally my anti-war feelings led me to walk away from the camp without permission. After five days of an alcoholic and drug haze, I wandered back to the Army base of my own free will. Once again my previous record saved me from a dishonorable discharge. I was sentenced to thirty days at hard labor and restricted to the base.

My first sergeant, a man of Mexican extraction, took a personal interest in me. Pointing his finger at me, Sgt. Cadena announced, "Kelton! I'm going to see that you get an honorable discharge!" And he watched me almost every minute.

The late spring Lousiana weather was hot and humid. Sgt. Cadena would sit in the shade, sipping iced tea, while I shoveled a wheelbarrow full of sand, pushed it fifty feet, then unloaded it and returned for another load. If I slowed down, it simply meant that I had to work longer — until the entire pile of sand had been moved. Tomorrow only meant that I began shoveling the wheelbarrow full of sand, and hauling the pile back where it had been the day before. We called it — behind Sgt. Cadena's back — "the Mexican dragline." If I finished the sandpile early, I still had to check in every hour until midnight to make certain I wasn't leaving the base. I was determined to prove my independence, however, so a couple of times I sneaked into town after midnight and got drunk, working the next day without sleep. The Army would never break *my* spirit!

At the end of the thirty days, Sgt. Cadena made me his personal driver so he could watch me. He was indeed determined that I would get an honorable discharge. I am very thankful today for such a man having contributed to my life. All that time, however, I persuaded other soldiers to bring me cough syrup or booze or drugs. Again and again I would sneak into town. After being caught once, Sgt. Cadena threatened me with three years at hard labor.

A clerk attached to the headquarters platoon was talking to me one day. He said, "I have access to everybody's exam scores. Out of all five thousand on this base, including the colonel — and he's a West Point graduate — *you* have the highest scores! What are you doing drunk all the time?"

What *was* I doing drunk all the time? I never really understood clearly, but I guess I was just like other drunks and drug addicts — I was trying to kill myself! It seems that "normal" people like living and fear dying, but drunks and drug addicts fear living and anticipate dying. Something inside was driving me; I couldn't relax. I wanted to forget everything, especially the fact that I had walked out on my wife and baby.

They told me I needed psychiatric help. The

Army psychiatrist talked with me about the anxiety that so dominated my behavior. He decided that I had been hyperactive as a child. That seemed reasonable, except that I had never felt this anxiety before the age of fifteen. The psychiatrist quickly recognized that I was playing games with him, and he suggested rather strongly that I would never change.

But I was insignificant to the U.S. Army. Everyone in our division — the 35th Engineers — knew we were headed for Vietnam. As our departure day neared, I planned to go AWOL again and protest the war. At the last moment an order came down that men with less than six months remaining in their tours of duty would not be required to go to Vietnam. My records were examined. After deducting the five days I was absent, I still had exactly five months and twenty-nine days left in my service. I missed the war by one day! The man who replaced me was later killed in Vietnam.

I phoned Mom to tell her my news. I should have known her reaction. "Praise the Lord! David, God is protecting you!" She made me so angry.

My final six months in the Army were laced with more troubles. Because I enjoyed drinking and gambling in the black section of town, I often

42

got into trouble with other white soldiers. It may have been this issue — I was too drunk to remember — that led me to start a fight with another soldier, in a *taxi* of all places! Five of us were returning to the base at three a.m., and the cab driver was drunk, too. I think I broke the nose of the soldier beside the driver, because blood was spurting all over the front seat. The driver stopped the cab, jumped out and started screaming, "You ain't gonna rob me!" He reached into his sock to pull out a big knife, but he was so drugged and excited that he cut a long gash up his leg. Then he found a gun somewhere and fired it in the air. We ran in all directions! Suddenly a bullet whistled over my head. My buddy and I dived into the woods and lay there until we went to sleep. In the morning we sneaked into the barracks, where we were told to report to a certain office. The other three soldiers were already there. There was talk of a court martial, which could have resulted in a dishonorable discharge for me. Again something was said — perhaps it was that I only had a couple of weeks remaining to serve — and they just let me go without punishment.

Two days before I was to be discharged, I was going to my locker, where I had hidden a fifth of gin — which was illegal — to celebrate, but I slipped on a wet floor and broke my ankle badly. I spent ninety days *extra* in the Army — peeling potatoes with a cast on my leg! I cursed the Army every way I could think, because the rules say a soldier cannot be discharged while under the care of a doctor.

In January 1966 I was finally discharged — honorably — and returned to Charlotte with a swollen, painful ankle which never fully healed. And I was angry! Mom's outspoken faith irritated me. My spirit was not broken in the least, but neither was hers. I should have known that this warfare wouldn't end until one of us died.

Chapter 4

Always Lucky!

After several months of drinking to alleviate the pain in my ankle, I found a job managing a pool hall, a place that was really a front for the local "syndicate." We peddled drugs, bootleg liquor, stolen goods, and anything else that was illegal. Later, I ran a house of prostitution for a year. Trying anything to get money, I often had lots of it. Over the next few years my arrest record was *five pages long*! Yet somehow I never served more than two or three days in jail.

My life style quickly became as violent as the people I associated with. Actually, it's a miracle that I never killed anybody, although I once shot a man and wounded him seriously. I carried a couple of guns most of the time, although often I would use a "mule" to hold such hardware. He'd carry my drugs, too. A "mule" is a teenager who is new to this kind of life, but is awed by the older "pros." My mule would always stick close in case I needed a gun, but if the police picked me up, I would be "clean." An occasional pat on the back would keep a mule happy for days.

One night a Black Muslim burst into my bootleg joint with a gun. He walked up to the black barmaid I had hired, pulled out a gun, stuck it in her stomach, and said he was going to kill her for working for a whitey. His nickname was Psycho, for good reason. He was already widely known for violence.

He didn't see me as I tiptoed up behind him, cocked my gun, and shoved it right in his ear. "Put that gun down or I'll kill you!" I shouted.

Psycho cursed me, and threatened again to kill the barmaid, but I had my gun forced into his ear quite painfully. For about five minutes we had a genuine "Mexican standoff." We cursed each other, threatened each other — but he knew if he so much as moved his head, my gun could go off. And his ear was hurting — badly. Finally Psycho dropped his gun and I threw him out of the place. That evening he returned, we had a big brawl, and I threw him out again.

Sometime later Psycho came to see me and we made up. In fact, we even joined together in some crime. Criminals are a strange bunch, and I was one of them.

Later I began another period of sobriety, determining to do better. With my electronics training in the Army, I was able to find a job as an engineer with Simplex Time Recording Company. The boss liked me, and I did a superior job — as usual. Customers spoke highly of me, and I stayed away from drugs and drank very little. Once again, however, I began to get anxious and depressed. The moods became darker, and finally I decided to commit suicide. "Why not do it the fast way?" I recalled a lonely stretch of railroad track where a big freight train came through every morning about three or four o'clock. Taking a handful of barbiturates and a bottle of liquor, I parked my new Buick convertible directly on the railroad tracks. While waiting for the crash, I took the pills, drank the booze, and passed out on the seat.

Mom had sensed all evening that something was seriously wrong with me, and she had gone to all the joints where she knew I usually hung out. Even though she had to go to work in the morning, she prayed and searched for hours, arriving home about two a.m. Getting undressed, she knelt to pray at the side of her bed. Suddenly, Mom saw the vision of a lonely, wooded area with a railroad crossing, and my car parked on the tracks.

Quickly Mom dressed again and jumped in her car. She knew exactly where that railroad crossing was located. Coming right to the very spot, she pushed me across the seat and drove my car home. Somehow she got me in the house and into bed.

"David," she announced a few hours later, "Jesus showed me where you were."

"Aw, Mom, how dumb do you think I am?" I knew Jesus was dead. How could a dead man show her where I was? Yet, how did she know?

A few days later I was drinking in a bar again, and the subject of cars came up. A loudmouthed guy said his Oldsmobile could outrun my Buick Wildcat, so we challenged each other to a race on the interstate highway. I had never been a fast driver, because my Dad had strictly coached me as a fourteen-year-old *not* to drive fast. Even at my worst, I drove normally. But this guy had really irritated me, so we headed out of town. I was doing 120 miles per hour with a friend in the seat beside me, and that Oldsmobile right behind. I started to pass two tractor-trailers, when a woman pulled out from between the trucks without looking. I slammed into her with a terrific crash. While I was trying to stop my car, the Oldsmobile smashed into my rear.

My convertible roof popped open and I was thrown over the windshield with my laced shoes still lying on the floor of the car. I bounced at least twenty-five feet on the highway in front of the car — yet I was hardly scratched! When I stood up and looked back, my car was on fire, and my friend was still inside. He was badly hurt, so I quickly pulled him out, burning my hands in the process. As I was dragging him away, my car exploded, then exploded again and again, actually being lifted into the air. The noises were deafening! The woman I had hit was pregnant, and she was extremely emotional. The man in the Oldsmobile was lying on the road, critically injured.

Ambulances took us to the hospital, where I called Mom. She phoned her family doctor, who stopped by to check on me. The police knew they had me for drunk driving this time, so they came to the hospital to arrest me. But Mom's doctor told them he had examined me, and he said I had not been drinking. Her doctor must have lied to the police, because I was loaded, although I could hold a lot of liquor without showing it. The cops were furious, but there was nothing they could do following the doctor's statement. The most the policeman could do was threaten me: "You'd better hope that woman doesn't lose her baby!" She didn't.

The next day Mom went to see the cars. They were all "totalled"! I had been planning to go to Myrtle Beach for that weekend, so Mom had

49

packed a little suitcase for me and put it in my trunk. The whole rear end of the car was burned, and the suitcase and everything in it were destroyed, except for a little Bible she had slipped inside. The Bible was completely intact amid the ashes, and Mom received new hope that God would change me.

But my drinking just increased again, until my boss finally fired me. He told me I was an alcoholic, and I needed help. I laughed at him, and said I wasn't an alcoholic and I didn't need any help!

So it was back to running another pool hall, with all the crime that went with that job. I felt miserable, hating myself and hating the world. I could hardly go to sleep at night, and I was sick when I woke up each day. The only thing that would make me feel better was another drink or some pills. My eating habits were terrible, and I looked emaciated. Sex was always readily available, but it became less and less enjoyable.

Someone asked me recently how I managed to survive an attack of the flu in those days. My answer was that I never knew when I caught any infectious disease — I felt as if I had the flu all the time. The alcohol and drugs caused the pain, yet I had to have them to dispel the anxiety within me and the guilt over having walked out on my wife and baby years before. For one day, at the least, alcohol and drugs could help me to forget it all.

Through the years I met a lot of big-time criminals. Many of them were quite intelligent, and I knew I was as smart as any of them. But I had no interest in such involvement. They were all greedy for money and power; I just wanted to get rid of that restless anxiety within me, so I never got involved in big operations.

Only one thing terrified me — jail! I couldn't stand it behind bars. Whenever I was picked up by the police, I became alarmed if they appeared to have a good case against me. Mom would pray each time, and each time something strange would occur, and I would be released. The cops were almost beside themselves with rage, but they couldn't do anything about it. I'd leave the courtroom happy, thinking how lucky I was.

Chapter 5

Brinda

As angry and depressed as I felt most of the time, I could feel a great tenderness for animals and abused people. Within a year after I was discharged from the Army, a young guy came into my pool hall with a tiny teenage girl who looked as bedraggled as anyone I had ever seen. She was wearing a man's jacket that hung nearly to her ankles. Her shoes were summer sandals, yet it was late autumn. When the weather turned cool in Charlotte, Brinda had stolen the jacket. She had run away from home in Georgia, and was working as a waitress in a restaurant down the street. I felt sorry for her.

Several weeks later Brinda's boyfriend was drafted into the Army. She looked so lonely and pathetic. When I asked this little girl how old she was, Brinda said she was eighteen, but I found out months later that she had lied to me.

I enjoyed flashing money around the

girls — when I had it. So I went to a dress shop and described Brinda to the clerk, returning with an armful of nice clothing.

"What are these for?"

"They're for you," I said.

Brinda was suspicious; nobody had ever done anything kind for her. "I'll pay you for them when I get the money," she stammered. All the clothing fit her perfectly.

Several weeks later Brinda's boyfriend came home from basic training. All of a sudden I felt strangely protective. I knew he planned to take her to bed, so I went with them to Brinda's little apartment. Her boyfriend didn't have the courage to try to throw me out, so I got drunk sitting on the couch. I picked that spot because there was no door to her bedroom, and I could see both of them lying in her bed. He never touched her all night!

Why was I acting like this, anyway? I didn't care about this kid! But as soon as that soldier returned to Fort Bragg, Brinda agreed to move in with me. "I'll sleep with you," she announced, "but I won't marry you!" She had been hurt too badly by a rough world, and she couldn't trust anybody.

I laughed at her. "That's good, because I don't ever intend to get married!" So I tried to get rid of her. We were determined to keep our distance from each other, yet I'd repeatedly take her in, and Brinda quickly began sticking close to me. Then somebody gave her a chance as a go-go dancer. She was very good at it, too. She admitted to me that her first job at age sixteen had been as a go-go dancer. No one had ever taught her to dance — she was a "natural."

I didn't really like Brinda, but she was clinging to me all the time. I was the first person who had ever been kind to her. I'd throw her out of my apartment, and a day-or-so later she'd be back. I just couldn't get rid of her. Brinda was like a little puppy; she smothered me with affection. I didn't like people getting that close to me, so once I hit her in the face, knocking her to the floor. She turned into a tigress! Grabbing a wine bottle from the floor, Brinda smashed the bottom of it and came at me with the jagged edges aimed for my face. I knocked her to the floor a second time, only to watch her get up and lunge at me with the broken bottle again. Finally I subdued her. A few minutes later she was all love and kisses.

Sometimes Brinda was so stubborn that she would "argue with a fence post." While living in a skid row hotel, she and I got into a violent argument. I was so angry at Brinda that I actually wanted to kill her. She recognized it, too. Out the door and down the hall she scampered; I was right behind. I had murder in my heart. Brinda turned the corner and ran down the next hall. I lurched around the corner — and ran right into the cleaning lady! The collision knocked her off her feet and broke her arm.

Again the cops loved it. Charging me with assault and battery and anything else they could think of, they felt they finally had me all but locked up for awhile. I made bail that evening, and was released until my hearing. Later that night I was arrested for fighting, and I made bail again. An hour-or-two later, I was locked up for public drunkenness, and I made bail once more. Jailed three times in one day, yet I walked out onto the streets. Once again — at the hearing — something strange happened, and I wasn't even sentenced. Lucky again!

Brinda had been so frightened of me when I tried to kill her that she didn't stop running until she jumped on a bus headed for Georgia. Yet three days later she was right back again. Sometimes when I'd throw her out, Brinda would move to a cheap apartment. But it didn't last long; like a little puppy she'd come in as soon as I'd let her.

One day Mom heard about Brinda, and that I had thrown her out. Mom came and got her, inviting Brinda to stay at her house. Brinda was astonished. "You mean you'd have a girl like *me* in your home?"

"Sure, honey. Jesus loves you!" It was a whole new experience for this battered little girl. A tragic victim of violent child abuse, Brinda would not leave me, no matter how badly I mistreated her. After that, whenever I would disappear, Mom and Brinda would often search for me together.

Sometimes I made big money — selling drugs or marketing stolen goods, perhaps shooting pool. I enjoyed flashing hundred-dollar bills, arrogantly discarding ones and fives on the floor. Brinda loved it. In fact, she seemed to admire almost everything I did. A few days later we were broke again.

One night Brinda and I were in the Beef 'n Rib Room, a well-known Charlotte center for crime. Lots of other people were there, too. Brinda had had too much to drink, and she was beginning to get sick. Suddenly the place was surrounded by police cars — I never saw so many in one place! They apparently thought they had a drug bust. Brinda hid my drugs where no cop would dare to look. The police were frisking all of us when Brinda started to vomit because of all the alcohol in her. A cop asked, "Which one is your guy?"

"That one!" She pointed me out.

He came and grabbed me: "Take her home!"

Every other man in the place was jailed that night! It was amazing!

One hot summer evening a friend and I were walking down the street, wondering how we could steal a few bucks for some booze. Passing a house with the door opened, we noticed a man watching television in his living room. We heard his phone ring, and we saw him go around the corner to answer it in the kitchen. My friend and I looked at each other, then quickly opened the screen door and slipped into his living room. The man was still talking in the kitchen, so we unplugged his TV set and quietly carried it out the door. Hurrying down to the VFW Club, we sold it for enough to buy a few more drinks. We both enjoyed a good laugh as we wondered what that guy thought when he returned to his living room.

I refused to allow anyone to get close to me. I preferred to keep my partners in crime at a safe distance. First, I didn't want to be hurt again — ever — by becoming too attached to another person. And, second, I didn't trust anyone else, least of all those I "worked" with. Most of the drug traffic in North Carolina at that time involved blacks, so I spent a lot of time doing illegal business with black people. There were several places in Charlotte where I was the only white man allowed. I was trusted.

"Snake" was an interesting black man. He was small, quick, energetic — and mean — with eyes that seemed to dart back and forth. From time to time Snake and I pulled some jobs together. I didn't really like him because he could be so violent. Snake was quite skilled with a knife. He thought nothing of killing another person, so I worked with him only when it seemed necessary. I told Brinda that if she ever got scared of anyone in my bootleg joint, she should sit down beside Snake: I knew nobody would start trouble around him. As with everyone else, I didn't trust Snake, and yet — strangely — I trusted him with my girlfriend.

I suppose I was almost as unpredictable as Snake. The arguments and threats that typify street people were not for me. Such talk was a sign of weakness. I never threatened; I never warned anyone — I just struck! Strong arms and a quick temper had been inherited from my grandfather. I could hit a man once, and he'd be on the floor.

On the streets you learn quickly how to "size up" a man. You must be able to estimate how strong he is, how stable he is, if he can be trusted, and what he thinks of you. And you must learn it quickly — or you're dead! The "sixth sense" of self-preservation becomes finely tuned. To this day that keen discernment I learned on the streets continues to help me.

59

When Snake didn't have enough money to make a big drug purchase, he'd come to me, and we would pool our resources. Then Snake and I would hang around the Beef 'n Rib Room and peddle our drugs. That would provide some money for a few more days of booze and pills for myself.

One afternoon I took three of my black friends into a "redneck" restaurant run by a crippled old Greek. This was a country music place where blacks were never seen. A tall, older white man I had noticed a few times came into the restaurant. Walking up to our booth, he asked belligerently, "Boy! What're you bringin' them niggers in here for?"

I stood up. "What did you say?"

"I said, 'Why're you bringin' them niggers in here?'"

Like a flash I hit him in the face. He tumbled to the floor, blood spurting from his nose. I was on him like a cat, beating him some more. Somehow he pulled a knife from his pocket and slashed me down the side of my face. I jumped up to get away from the knife. Then I put my tongue in my cheek — and it came out the other side! Enraged, I reached in my belt for my pistol, grabbed a clip from the lefthand pocket and inserted it quickly. But he saw the gun and ran for the street. I started

60

firing at him! Two or three of my bullets struck the doorway a split second after he rounded the corner.

Customers hit the floor like falling bricks. The old Greek hobbled from behind the cash register, screaming at me. My black friends found a towel and held it on my cheek, which was bleeding profusely. I just stood there and cursed that I had missed that so-and-so.

Then we heard the police siren. Turning on the proprietor, I pointed my gun at him and threatened, "Old man, if you tell the cops anything, I'll kill you!" He believed me.

Two policemen burst in the door and asked me what happened. "I dunno. Some guy came in here and slashed me with a knife."

"Who was he?"

"I dunno. Never saw him before." My eyes were as blank as could be.

"Can you give me a description of him?"

"I never got a look at him. He just came in and slashed me."

"You know this guy with the knife?" a cop demanded of the proprietor.

"N-n-no, sir! Never saw him before." He was trembling.

"Anybody else know that guy?"

"No suh!" echoed around the restaurant.

A big black cop took me to the hospital in his squad car. I couldn't believe it: he never frisked me! Possession of the pistol wedged inside my belt would have put me in jail. An intern sewed me up and I was out in thirty minutes, sporting a three-inch scar that I carry to this day. As this black policeman drove me back downtown, he asked, "Why'd you get in that fight?"

"Because he called my friends 'niggers'!"

I made another friend that night.

Chapter 6

Journey to Disaster

Slowly my mind and my body began to deteriorate as the result of continual drinking and taking drugs. My liver and my kidneys were both failing. At times I would wake up wondering where I was and how I got there. These blackouts became longer and more frequent. I wasn't sober enough to be trusted to handle a pool hall or bootleg joint. Sinking into the mire of being a common "wino," food meant very little to me, and sex was almost impossible. My friends became tired of lending me money, and I could no longer hold a cue stick steady enough to win money at shooting pool. Perhaps I would work several days on a construction job, use the money to buy large quantities of cheap wine, and then black out for a period. I began talking to myself. Then came the hallucinations. Petty crime was as much as I seemed capable of accomplishing — just enough to buy some more booze. I was sick all the time. The end seemed to be nearing.

About that time Mom and Brinda decided to do something drastic. They came to get me in the skid row hotel where I was living. I was out of money, and Mom said, "We're going to get help for you." To me, "help" meant getting rid of the terrible pain and sickness, so I stumbled out with them. As they led me to the street to get into Mom's car, I went into a convulsion. Mom drove me to her house, where I had another convulsion on the sidewalk. I was trying to swallow my tongue. Running into the house, Mom called the Prayer Tower at Oral Roberts University. The woman who answered in Tulsa had been an alcoholic herself, and she told Mom that I could die if she didn't get some alcohol in me. Mom was so desperate that she violated her lifelong principles, quickly purchasing the first bottle she could grab in the liquor store. She and Brinda poured some of the whiskey in me, and slowly I regained consciousness.

Mom gently told me about a home for alcoholics in Greensboro. I was feeling so miserable that I agreed to go. While Mom went to the telephone to make arrangements, I found the bottle she had just purchased, and I finished it off. By the time Mom had it all settled, I was feeling fine again; in fact, I was getting high.

"I'm not going!" I announced.

No matter how much Mom and Brinda

pleaded with me, I was not going to go. So Mom called my cousin Terry Sue. Her husband Bill was a muscular construction worker, standing about six feet, three inches tall, weighing at least 215 pounds, and he's a gentle giant of a Christian. He came to the house and tried pleasantly to get me to go. When I refused, Bill laid his big hands on me, put me on the floor, and tied my hands behind my back. Then he tied my feet together and threw me in the back seat of Mom's car. Bill drove us to Greensboro. Brinda sat with my head in her lap, trying to comfort me in spite of my cursing and complaining.

Hope Harbor was established by the Rev. John Stephenson, a Spirit-filled Presbyterian and a former alcoholic himself. I was taken into a large reading room where several men were playing games or reading or talking among themselves. I was a mess. Wearing only a T-shirt, jeans and old shoes, I hadn't had a bath in weeks, and I reeked from my own vomit. I hadn't shaved in days, and my hair was long and dirty. When asked how long it had been since I had eaten, I had no idea. I was cursing everyone, and demanding to be released. I told them I didn't want their help, and started to get violent. Bill subdued me again. They brought a drink and told me to swallow it, but I refused. Brinda said it was a mixed drink, so I swallowed it, only to realize that it was "mixed" raw eggs, honey and other nutritious things.

After being dragged into another room, I was forcibly strapped to a bed. So began my experience of detoxification. For several days I went through hell-on-earth. Sick and vomiting, cursing and screaming, I suffered torment that is indescribable. When the most violent of the sickness finally subsided, I was too weak to get out of bed.

After five days I was able to stand, but my legs were wobbly. I felt like a newborn calf, unsure of each step. Going up and down the stairs to the dining room was almost more than I could accomplish. After I got to the table, I couldn't hold the silverware steady enough to get the food to my mouth. My hands shook so badly that I would drop the food all over me. Drinking coffee was impossible until someone showed me how to put a towel around my neck, holding the ends with both hands. I could then push forward with my hands and hold the coffee cup still enough to drink it.

Rev. Stephenson called me into his office and explained the rules to me. If I ever drank alcohol, I would automatically be expelled. I had to go to their church services each Sunday morning and every evening — eight times a week! I shuddered. After I got strong enough, I wouldbe expected to work in one of their second-hand stores.

The daily services were held by volunteers from various churches of the Greensboro area. All the preachers seemed to have the same message: I was a bad person who was headed for hell unless I became a Christian. I thought if I were to become a Christian and read the Bible, all I would find there was fire and brimstone. I needed someone to speak "peace" to me; all I had known for years was anxiety. Could hell really be worse? The Army psychiatrist had long ago told me that I was incorrigible. Doctors and police said there was no hope for me. Once a junky, always a junky. Once an alcoholic, always an alcoholic. I needed peace, and I needed hope.

One Saturday afternoon a pastor and several couples from his church came to visit Hope Harbor, bringing crafts for us to assemble — ceramic ashtrays and basket weaving kits. I asked, "Tell me, preacher, if I make this ashtray and weave this basket, will that stop me from robbing people and taking dope and drinking booze? Will this make me okay?"

"Well," he answered hesitantly, "it'll take your mind off your problems, you know."

"I don't need no basket or ashtray. I can do that by getting drunk!"

The women were embarrassed and began walking away, leaving only the minister. He stammered a little.

I looked at him and demanded, "Is this the Church's answer to crime and alcoholism? Just weave a little basket or make a little ashtray, and everything will work out?"

"Well, I don't know what to say to you," he answered. "I want to help you."

"Then help me!" I insisted. "Tell me what to do."

"You'll have to stop your drinking and drugs and involvement in crime," the pastor responded, obviously quite uncomfortable. "I think you can be helped."

"Preacher, if I could stop drinking and drugs, I wouldn't be here! I thought your big God and all you people had some kind of answer for me! Can't you do something, and then I can live happily ever after?"

He lowered his head and muttered, "I'm sorry. I don't know what to say to you." The pastor turned and walked away in embarrassment.

After more than six weeks of daily services — about fifty in all — I decided that these church people are a bunch of phonies; they don't have any power at all!

I was sent to work in a second-hand store. Seeing a lot of old TV sets there, I began to tinker with them. None of them worked properly —

that's why they had been donated. Soon I had most of them functioning, and Hope Harbor began to profit from the sales of those television sets. They were of much more value than the old clothes and furniture.

One weekend Mom and Brinda came to see me. I had been at Hope Harbor for more than a month. I finally realized that I loved Brinda and needed her. For the first time in nearly fifteen years, I wanted to be close to someone who loved me. I had occasionally thought about asking her to marry me, but it wouldn't make sense for her to marry a wino, so I never made any serious plans. Now I felt I could make a living, doing television repairs. On Sunday I asked Brinda to marry me. She was so happy. Mom was thrilled, too. At last she could feel as if her prayers were being heard.

I worked on those old TV sets in earnest. The following Saturday, Rev. Stephenson called me into his office. "David, your rehabilitation is going quite well. You're not causing any trouble. You've shown that you have a lot of ability by fixing those TV sets. I'm real proud of you."

Funny how I'd heard that story before! Time and again I had heard similar words of praise, only to foul up my life each time. I thanked Rev. Stephenson for the compliment.

Then he told me how he used to be an

alcoholic, and how God had saved him from that life. He continued, "Those TV sets are starting to sell, and it's helping Hope Harbor's finances a great deal. Now here's five dollars to buy yourself some cigarettes, and to make you feel as if you're accomplishing something."

I thanked him and walked out the door with a five dollar bill in the pocket of the nice clothes they had given me. I was twenty-eight years old, sober, thinking about getting married, and . . . well, maybe there would be a nice future for me yet. I started down the street with the key to freedom in my pocket — five dollars.

Then I started thinking. I'm no good. I walked out on my family — all I've ever done is hurt them. The awful guilt of abandoning my wife and baby welled up within me. I could hear the psychiatrist, the doctors, the police: "All you'll ever be is a junky, a drunk!" So I walked into a convenience store and spent all the money on four fifths of cheap wine.

I carried the sack full of wine back to Hope Harbor and sat down behind the hedge outside the chapel window. No one could see me as I opened the first bottle and drank it all. The sun went down and the lights went on. I knew it was time for the church service, so I listened through the open window as some visiting preacher was telling me how bad I was. "This place is crazy!" I thought. "They're just a bunch of squares! They ain't got no answers! They don't help anybody! Ashtrays and baskets! Fooey!" And I finished off another bottle.

"It must be close to ten o'clock," I thought. "The guys are starting to go upstairs. I've got to get inside before lights out." Hiding the rest of the wine in the hedge, I slipped in the front door. Like most alcoholics, I tried to act as if I weren't drunk. Nobody can tell it, I thought, forgetting that I hadn't had a drink in six weeks. It must have showed.

Rev. Stephenson called across the room: "David! Come here!" I strolled over to him as casually as I could. There was such a hurt look in his eyes. "David, you know the rules here. There will be no drinking in God's house. Get your things together. You're leaving now!" I think his heart was broken.

"Well, I was thinkin' 'bout leavin' anyhow," I slurred. "This is a dumb place!" I gathered what little I had and walked out the door to retrieve the partial bottle of wine in the bushes.

"Hey, Kelton!" I looked up to see a fellow standing on the sidewalk. "Where're you going?"

"Who are you?"

71

"I'm Mike. Remember me? They just threw me out of there for drinking."

"Yeah! Me too!" I responded. "They're just a bunch of squares, anyhow!"

"Know where we can get something to drink?"

"Well, I've got some wine hidden in the hedge." So together we drank the rest of it.

Mike started laughing. "You know, Dave, my mother talked me into coming to this dump. She's just praying and praying that I'll see the light." And he laughed some more.

"Yeah, I know. My Mom's been praying for me for years." Somehow I didn't feel like laughing about it. I only wanted more to drink. I gotta forget!

"Dave! You know where we can get some money?"

"Yeah!" I boasted. "I got lots of connections in Charlotte. If we can get there, I can get money and booze and pills. I'll get some guns, too. I got lots of friends there." Just a common drunk, bragging about all my connections, when I knew quite well that none of my friends trusted me any longer. I had already borrowed far beyond their willingness to lend. But I had to act important in front of Mike.

"I got my car here," he volunteered. "I know where I can borrow some money for gas." I jumped in with Mike, and he drove to a house where he knew somebody. He came out a few minutes later with a bottle of beer for me. Another house produced some more wine. Finally he found a friend who gave him a fistful of pills and money for gas. We split the pills and I swallowed them without even checking what they were. Mike filled the tank with gas, and we headed down I-85 on that fateful journey to Charlotte, ninety miles to the south. The pills began taking effect, so I crawled into the back seat and passed out.

Half an hour later the two cars exploded into each other!

Chapter 7

Can a Dead Man Work a Miracle?

I don't understand it. Both of our mothers were praying, but Mike died and I lived. *Five* people died! Why was I chosen to live?

More strange things happened. That night a woman from the Garr Memorial Church in Charlotte was awakened suddenly with the terrible sensation of being crushed. Alarmed, she began to pray in tongues, and a voice said, "Pray for David." Not knowing who "David" was, she continued to pray while this awful crushing sensation persisted. She prayed earnestly for "David" for an hour-and-a-half. At the very moment the Iron Claw ripped the smashed car open, my left leg was freed from the weight of the engine and transmission — about forty miles to the north. Immediately the crushing sensation lifted from her body, and she knew that "David" — whoever he was — would be all right. She found her answer by reading the newspaper the next afternoon.

I was rushed to Rowan County Hospital, but they could do little for me there. It was decided that if I lived long enough to get to Charlotte Memorial Hospital, I might have a chance to make it. In Charlotte the examinations revealed the following damage: a broken neck, four broken ribs, lacerations all over my body, a broken left arm, a broken right hip, a broken right thigh bone, and a mangled left leg from the crushing by the engine; my jawbone was broken in five places, the roof of my mouth was split in two, part of my nose had been ripped loose and lost, teeth were imbedded into my skull, the left eyeball was torn loose (a surgeon later told me that my face looked like the windshield of a car that had been smashed with a baseball bat), and I had *massive* internal injuries, any one of which could have taken my life for days. Yet I was still breathing!

A total of seventeen doctors worked on me during the next two weeks — all of them expecting me to die at any moment. My blood pressure was too high for the instrument to record. I must have been suffering terribly, but mercifully I remained unconscious for most of those two weeks.

Brinda and Mom could hardly bear to look at me. Mom rallied her prayer warriors, and slowly I began to have periods of consciousness. A reconstruction specialist operated on me twice, lifting what was left of my face and totally rebuilding my skull. He put me back together with silicone and wire. There was no chance to save my left eye, but the surgeon did what he could for it.

The pain was unbearable, and because of my years of drug abuse, the doctor had to administer near-lethal doses of pain killers merely to give me a little relief. So there I was — high on drugs again! The pain was still excruciating!

Another of those strange things occurred a few days after the wreck. During my most critical period, a traveling evangelist named J. Herman Alexander experienced a strong urgency to return home to Charlotte. Herman was holding revival meetings in California, when suddenly he became aware that something was seriously wrong in Charlotte. He immediately cancelled his revival meetings and flew home. Surprised to discover that nothing was wrong with his elderly mother, the evangelist pondered this strange urgency he had felt in California. As he prayed further, he sensed that he should go to Charlotte Memorial Hospital. Mom recognized him as he was wandering through the hall, so she asked Herman to stop and pray for her son David.

"That's the reason I'm here!" the evangelist abruptly announced. Herman Alexander immediately walked with assurance into the intensive care unit, where he laid his hands on me and began to pray. I don't recall it, but my brother Tim said I began to cry, then lapsed into unconsciousness again. Rev. Alexander looked at Tim and said, "He's going to be all right now." And the evangelist walked out as mysteriously as he had come in, satisfied that he had accomplished everything that God had sent him all the way across the nation to do.

A few days later, new X-rays showed no broken neck and no broken bone in my left arm! All those massive internal injuries were healed, too! And my left eye is fine to this day. The doctors were fascinated and bewildered. Being so sedated, I was unaware of all these miraculous healings. I didn't believe my family when they told me about it later. "These Christians!" I thought. "Always opportunistic!"

But the pain! For about six weeks I was wishing I *had* died in the wreck. With my head wrapped, I lived in total darkness and terrible agony. No comfort, no understanding, no hope, and no relief from unbearable suffering — I think I know what hell is like. Sometimes Christians would come to the hospital and pray for me and sympathize with me. But one of my relatives came to tell me how she wished I had died and gone to hell — I had disgraced the family and caused my mother so much heartache. Even though I was crippled, bedfast and blind, I could still hate. I developed an intense hatred toward that relative. Most people, however, were nice to me. Without Brinda's love and compassion, though, I couldn't have survived. I think I would have gone crazy. She and Mom practically lived at the hospital for several weeks — and they were both working at full-time jobs.

Six weeks after the accident I was discharged, filled with pain, but healing rapidly. The hospital staff were shaking their heads in disbelief. They knew they had seen a miracle, but I denied it all.

I told Brinda we were going to get married. Mom had been enthusiastic before, but now she felt Brinda shouldn't marry a cripple. Brinda would willingly accept me — crippled or whole. I insisted, so Mom reluctantly cooperated. Her pastor, however, refused to marry us because I had been divorced. Mom then asked her brother-in-law, the principal of the Christian school, and he agreed to marry us. But, two days before the wedding, my uncle had to leave town on an emergency trip. Finally, Mom found a young minister just out of Bible college. After Mom's assurances that we truly loved each other and would stay married — "After all, they've been living together for several years!" — the youthful minister agreed.

My aunt and uncle allowed us to use their

home for our Sunday afternoon wedding. My cousin Terry Sue and her husband, "Big Bill," agreed to stand with us as matron of honor and best man. But the wedding was delayed two hours because Bill had fallen asleep at home. Finally, someone pushed me in a wheelchair into the large living room, where everyone was having a good time except me. I was doing this for Brinda, and she loved it. But I hurt all over, I thought the whole ceremony was silly, and I had already waited two hours. Mom told me to stand up on my crutches when Brinda walked down the hall. It was the first time I had stood on my feet since the accident. The preacher asked Brinda to repeat her vows, then he looked at me. I was "as white as a ghost." All the blood seemed to rush from my brain. This was the youthful minister's first wedding, and he panicked when he saw my face. He forgot the normal words, and blurted out, "Do you love this girl?"

I whispered weakly, "I do."

"ThenIpronounceyoumanandwife! Sit down!" And I collapsed into the wheelchair. If that young man had asked me, "Wilt thou . . .?" I could truthfully have answered, "I wilt!"

My family was so good to me. My brother Tim had recently completed Bible college and accepted the pastorate of a small Pentecostal congregation in Charlotte. He and his new wife Claudia took Mom and Brinda and me to Myrtle Beach, and we all celebrated the wedding together. My family loved me so much, and I had only hurt them. Each time I was sober, they'd think I had changed. And each time I would crush those hopes. Now I was sober again, but not of my own choice. I couldn't go anywhere without someone to help me. And no one would take me to a liquor store.

Living in Mom's house was terribly confining. She was *always* talking about Jesus. She and Brinda would work side-by-side in the kitchen — arguing all the time. I cursed Mom, and told her to keep her religion to herself. Brinda would listen to Mom, then dispute everything she said about God. Brinda would argue with anybody! Neither of us wanted her Jesus, but Mom loved us anyhow — and kept right on talking about Jesus! And there I was — a captive audience, stuck in a wheelchair, with my body wracked with pain! On the other hand, I hated those lonely daytime hours while Mom and Brinda were at their jobs. The anxiety sometimes seemed as bad as the physical pain. If I could only get out of this house!

My body continued to heal until the surgeon finally removed the leg cast six months after the accident. I hobbled around on crutches, then graduated to a cane. The doctor prescribed a built-up shoe to allow for the 2⅛ inches missing from my left leg. Continuing to improve under the physical therapy program at the hospital, at last I could have some freedom!

I would hobble in that enormous shoe down the street to the bus stop and ride downtown to the Beef 'n Rib, where I began drinking, shooting pool and gambling again. Brinda willingly gave me money for booze. Her boss at the restaurant provided her with free liquor, and she thought I should have the same privilege, too. Mom got angry because we wouldn't help pay the bills, yet I'd squander everything Brinda earned at the restaurant. Neither of us felt a responsibility for buying any of the groceries.

A friend named John tried to interest me in his Alcoholics Anonymous chapter. I agreed, but every time he came to take me to the meeting, I was too drunk to go. Finally I did go to one AA meeting with him. John offered me a job in the construction business. It was almost a joke. I was still so weak that I could hardly stand, yet John was patient. Gradually my strength returned, and I was able to do some concrete work for him in spite of having to drag my left leg. Walking up stairs was still quite difficult, and could only be accomplished with great effort and pain.

Mom thought she could see some softening in me, and I guess she was right. Tim tried to be a pastor to me, although I would have none of it. Yet there *was* a little change in me. I found myself *wanting* to believe in Mom's Jesus, although I knew Jesus was only a myth! Jesus wasn't real: He was dead! Weak, gullible people seemed to need this myth in order to make it through life. I guess it was the persistent *love* of so many Christians that was softening me. Mom accepted every tiny sign of change in me with renewed hope, but I'd always go right back to my old ways. Maybe the authorities were right: I was a drunk, a junky, a criminal, a violent man—and that's all I'd ever be.

After nearly a year in Mom's house, Brinda and I couldn't stand her preaching any longer. We found a tiny furnished apartment, but soon got thrown out for non-payment of rent. I was spending all of our money on booze! Back to Mom's! She'd always take us in! I was drunk nearly all the time, so we weren't able to stay in any furnished apartment very long.

At last we ended up in one room in a cheap hotel on Trade Street — the skid row section of Charlotte. Without cooking privileges, Brinda did most of her eating at the restaurant where she was the cook on the day shift. Her boss liked her

83

because she was a hard worker, even allowing her to fix a free meal for me each day. I really wasn't interested in food, but if either of us got hungry at any other time of the day, we'd patronize the hotel's soft drink and candy machines. My body was deteriorating all over again.

One day Mom asked me to go to a "meeting" with her. The meeting was at the White House Inn — right down the street from the flophouse where Brinda and I were living. At least it wasn't a church, so we agreed. Mom, Tim, Claudia and I went together; I insisted that we sit in the rear, near the door.

These were strange people, beginning with their name: Full Gospel Businessmen's Fellowship International. They were hugging each other, and singing a silly song with all kinds of body movements — it seemed to be a children's song — "His Banner over Me Is Love." I sat impatiently through long testimonies and a sermon. In my mind I was mocking everything they were doing. A man who said he was a dairy farmer from California was introduced as the President. A *farmer* at the head of a businessmen's organization? That seemed silly, too. His name was Demos Shakarian.

Demos was asked to close the meeting with prayer. Finally it would be over! But he stopped abruptly: "Wait a moment! God has just spoken to me! There is someone here who has a short leg. If you will come up to the stage right now, God is going to heal you."

I can hardly recall anything that was said that evening. It's almost a blank in my memory. The first thing I remember clearly was realizing I was clomping toward the front of the ballroom with Tim right behind. I honestly do not recall getting out of my chair. When I got to the stage, Demos Shakarian told me to sit in one of the empty metal chairs. Then he asked me how short my left leg was.

I responded, "2⅛ inches."

Suddenly this dairy farmer from California bowed his head and spoke three electric words: "Jesus! Heal him!"

I was paralyzed! For a few moments I couldn't seem to move at all. The muscles of my left leg began to twitch and jerk. It was hurting as if I had a muscle cramp. Then the leg shot straight out! I was terrified! Jumping out of the chair, I found myself standing lopsided. With the built-up shoe, my left leg was now much longer than the other one.

When I dropped to the floor to take off my shoes, the crowd thought God had knocked me down. But in seconds I was back on my feet, and

I was standing perfectly straight! Both legs were exactly the same length! Everyone stood up and began praising God excitedly. The noise was deafening!

I had never been so scared in all my life! Those fateful words still echoed in my head: "Jesus! Heal him!" In an instant I knew Jesus was not a myth — He was real! And He had power! Worse yet, He was not only *alive*, but He knew my address! Jesus knew exactly where I was! He who I thought was the subject of human superstition — the One who wasn't real because I couldn't see Him — actually caused my leg to grow $2\frac{1}{8}$ inches — in a moment of time! I couldn't see Him, yet I knew He was there — and in power! I had never before experienced real power in a Christian service. It was a terrifying moment for this hardheaded atheist!

Tim led me back to Mom and Claudia amid a tremendous chorus of praise. Everybody was happy except me. Only by sheer will power did I restrain myself from running out of the building. "Let's get out of here!" I demanded.

We walked out into the rain. "David!" Mom said. "You can't walk in the rain with no shoes! Come on home with us!"

"I'm going back to my place!"

Since I refused to go home with them, Tim suggested that we stop in a nearby all-night restaurant for something to eat. I finally agreed. We walked up the steps into the restaurant. Mom cried out, "David! You're walking up the steps!"

"Uh . . . yeah!" I wasn't thrilled at all.

Tim and Claudia and Mom praised the Lord as we hurried in from the rain. I must have looked stupid, carrying my shoes with my socks soaking wet. We sat down, but I was too nervous to remain quiet.

"I gotta go!"

"David!" they all pleaded in unison. "Please come home!" Tim tried to stop me, but I was so scared and so jittery, I just couldn't sit still. I picked up my wet shoes and hurried out into the midnight rain.

I sloshed along the wet sidewalk to the nearest joint, laid my shoes on the bar, and proceeded to get drunk!

After the first drink, I decided the healing was all a dream, so I pinched myself. Realizing I wasn't asleep, I needed another drink. Then I decided that Shakarian-fellow had *hypnotized* me. I got off the bar stool and stood in my wet socks — still perfectly straight. The built-up shoe was staring at me from the bar, and that revelation required a third drink. It was spooky! That Jesus — if He's down the street in the White House Inn, I wonder if He's in this bar, too? I gotta quit thinking! And so I drank and drank until I was oblivious of my new problem — Jesus!

Chapter 8

"I Hate Miracles"

Did this miracle change me? Not really. Well, yes, it did, in a way. My friends would be drinking in a bar, when I might say, "You know, I think I'm a Christian."

"Whaddaya mean, you're a Christian?" And everybody would laugh.

"Well, Jesus healed my leg. You know how crippled I was. I didn't believe in Him before, and now I do." One drunk would nod his head in agreement, while another would laugh. Then we'd all engage in a truly-stupid theological discussion. But I knew what I knew: formerly I had not believed in Jesus, and now I did! Like Him or not, He was real!

The petty crime, the odd jobs, the restlessness, the drinking and drugs, the constant sickness and pain — all these were still very much a part of my life. But now that I was supposed to be a Christian, that meant I had to go to church! And so I did! Sunday after Sunday I listened to Tim's sermons. I went to Bible study, but the next day I might be on drugs and rob somebody again. The cycle seemed endless. I'd go to Alcoholics Anonymous, get a temporary job in construction work (I was good at drywall construction), try to read the Bible, listen to everybody's advice, and then get discouraged and load up on drugs. I would take "speed" for a few days and go without sleep for as much as a week. This would be followed by a period of deep depression.

I had great difficulty understanding and accepting my leg healing, but the whole event seemed to go right past Brinda. She hardly noticed the miracle, and refused to discuss it. Tim's wife Claudia, however, made a great impression on Brinda. The two girls were the same age. Claudia was a young lady, and Brinda wanted to be like her. After my healing, when Tim and Claudia invited us to live in their home, Brinda begged me to go. I reluctantly gave in.

Claudia saw Brinda as crude, lazy and untidy. But slowly she realized that Brinda was totally untrained; she had no sense of responsibility because it had never been instilled in her. Certainly I had been no help. So Claudia demanded that Brinda assist with the cleaning and the kitchen work. Claudia also taught her personal cleanliness and neatness. Whereas Brinda would have "smart-mouthed" Mom and argued with her, she accepted everything Claudia told her. She still didn't want to hear about Jesus though — even from me.

Tim accepted me as his personal project. Terry Sue's husband cooperated by offering me a construction job, taking me back even after I would disappear for several days. Everyone encouraged me to stick with Alcoholics Anonymous. At the end of a year I even earned the "blue chip" from AA for being sober one full year. That was a joke! Not even Tim was aware of the times I was drunk because I avoided my family during those periods. Actually, I had merely "switched brands" — most of the time I was taking drugs instead of booze. I really wanted to do better, and I tried. But something inside was always driving me, keeping me restless and ill-at-ease. So whenever I weakened, I'd do it behind Tim's back. He was so kind to me, thinking that I was better. Tim even gave me a role in his church's Christmas play two months after the healing of my leg. I'd try everything Tim and other Christians suggested, hoping that each suggestion would give me peace and contentment. But these qualities were elusive. I was actually more miserable than ever before.

Finally I gave up on God. I just couldn't stand the pressure of this "game" any longer. I told Brinda we were getting out of Tim's house.

The next several months were the worst of all. I became harder than ever before — almost like a wild animal. Enraged, I got in several serious fights, and I hurt some guys real bad. My life seemed to be filled with more violence than ever. I wasn't necessarily involved in all the violence — it would just happen around me. I watched unconcerned as one guy beat his girlfriend badly in front of a number of people; nobody else cared either.

One of my friends who was good at shooting pool stopped his car in front of a bar where we were drinking, telling his wife and baby that he'd be right out. He came in only to buy a drink, but somebody challenged him to a five-dollar game of pool, and he couldn't resist the chance to make a quick five bucks. Instead of winning the game, he lost — and he had no money. Telling the winner that he wasn't going to pay him, my friend walked out the door to get in his car. The other guy ran out behind him and shot him in the back and killed him, splattering his blood all over his wife and baby in the car. I merely shrugged my shoulders.

I began running around with worse criminals than ever before. I traveled over Virginia and the

Carolinas — doing confidence games, "flim-flamming" trusting people out of their money. We'd use a local prostitute as a decoy to seduce a traveling businessman. Then we'd skip with his billfold. He'd be so embarrassed that he wouldn't report us to the police. It worked beautifully every time.

Periodically, I'd sober up and work for my cousin's husband for a few weeks. He was so patient with me! He had also hired a young converted hippie named David Rowell. This kid was always joyful, always singing praises to God. I figured it was all a phony act, so one day I pushed a seventy-pound concrete slab on his foot. David grabbed his foot and began hopping around in great pain — still praising the Lord! He really impressed me.

But inevitably I'd return to the streets. The blackout periods started again — and increased. One day I woke up on a living room couch and wandered around the house, wondering where I was. Nobody was at home. I had the feeling that whoever lived in this house was at church, although I didn't know what day it was. I walked outside to discover that I was in a black section of Charlotte. Somehow I managed to find my way home. Another time I woke up in a town in South Carolina, with no idea of how I'd gotten there.

Mom always asked preachers to pray that her son would quit drinking. One day she made that request of a traveling evangelist. He exploded, "Lady! If God would answer that prayer, your son would die of thirst! Drinking's not his problem! You've got to pray the *devil* out of him!"

Mom was shocked at his response! But slowly she began to understand what that evangelist had said, and her prayers changed. Alcohol was *not* my problem. She began zeroing in on her target.

By this time I'd use anything I could find to get high. I even began taking "cocktails" — shooting various drugs (not heroin) with a needle. After days on "speed" — during which I would rob people, fight and go without sleep — I suffered incredible depression. Each time I tried to relieve the depression with alcohol.

I was also supplying some well-known criminals with drugs. One night I was waiting for a sale on a corner, just down Trade Street from the White House Inn, where God healed my leg. Cops from the vice squad stuck a gun in my back: "Okay, David, put your hands on the lamppost!" They all knew me by name. "We got you this time!" They shook me down and found a lot of "speed."

That same night the Charlotte police arrested a girl named Morgana. She was well known across

94

the nation for publicity stunts, including jumping in a swimming pool with the mayor of Atlanta. Morgana has a very prominent bosom and always makes the most of it. At the same time I was arrested, the police were putting Morgana in jail for "indecent exposure." We came to trial the same day.

I was quite alarmed for two reasons. First, the cops had a good case against me. Second, I drew a magistrate known as "the hanging judge" because he never showed any mercy. He simply sent everyone to jail. I tried to get a different judge, but it didn't work. I knew I was headed for prison, so I prepared my mind to accept it. I didn't know if I could survive a long prison term.

Tim heard about my arrest, so he came to the trial to try to help me. Morgana drew the same judge, and she was in fine form that day. The news photographers and television cameras were all there. Morgana was displaying her figure for the reporters, and Tim unexpectedly got in the pictures on the evening TV news. He was so embarrassed! The judge was quite distracted by Morgana; in fact, he could hardly take his eyes off her. The courtroom had a circus atmosphere.

My case came up first. The judge collected himself and said, "David, they tell me that you could be anything you want to be. You don't have to live this way. What's wrong with you?"

"I don't know, sir."

"I don't understand people like you. It appears that the worst enemy you have is you, yourself." All this time Morgana was doing her best to distract the judge.

"Yes, sir." I was standing meekly before him, with my hands behind my back, waiting for the awful sentence.

"Well, I think I'll put you in prison for five years. Maybe you'll learn something. And then again, maybe you won't." He wrote something on the paper in front of him. Then the judge paused.

"I don't know why I'm doing this," he muttered. "It doesn't make any sense. But I am going to give you another chance. Instead of sentencing you to jail, I'm going to stipulate that you not break any law in the State of North Carolina for five years. Do you understand this?"

"Yes, sir."

"If you even break one law, I'm going to have you brought back to my court, and I'm going to give you the maximum sentence. I mean anything! — even a traffic violation! Is that clear?"

"Yes, sir. I understand."

"Dismissed!" And the judge proceeded to a much more interesting case.

I couldn't believe it! Neither could Tim! He was praising the Lord, and I was thinking how lucky I'd been. As I said, my arrest record was five pages long, but again — as usual — I was not sentenced.

Leaving the courthouse, I walked down the street and met a friend who had some "speed." We went in a nearby bar and drank beer and popped pills. Within a mere ten minutes I was already violating the judge's order!

I was so miserable! Repeatedly I'd wake up during the night in a cold sweat — shaking all over. I'd hear those words again and again: "Jesus, heal him!" I'd see my left leg being lengthened again and again! Only booze or drugs could relieve my terrible fear of this Jesus who had healed my leg. It was much easier to live the life of a common wino than to have experienced the power of the risen Lord Jesus Christ! Every sober moment now was a moment of terror, so I didn't stay sober very much. Slowly my skin was turning yellow from my deteriorating liver and kidneys. And I didn't really care! I just didn't care!

One night I was sitting in a bootleg joint,

drinking. The black woman who owned the place got in a violent argument with someone. She grabbed a twelve-gauge shotgun and whirled around to shoot this guy. Her aim was poor, and she missed him. The blast went right past my face, shattering the window beside me. I was told later (I was so drunk I didn't recall it) that I merely looked at the broken window and took another drink.

Once I had shorted a guy on a drug deal, and he was furious. He found me in the Beef 'n Rib. Pointing his pistol at me, he said he was going to kill me for cheating him.

"Go ahead!" I taunted him. "Pull the trigger!"

He cursed me some more, shaking the gun barrel in front of my face. "I'm going to kill you for beating me out of that money!"

I looked at him without a bit of expression in my face: "You don't have guts enough to pull that trigger!" And he didn't. I was sort of hoping he *would* shoot me. That would solve a lot of problems, I figured.

One evening my uncle and several men from his church came to our little apartment. They announced that God had sent them to pray for me. I had been taking pills and booze for days, and I was so sick, so full of pain. I mocked them and cursed them. They told me I was full of demons and they were going to cast them out of me. When they tried to pray, I started swinging, and drove them out of the apartment.

The incident left me so unnerved that I had to have a drink. But we were broke because I'd already spent all of Brinda's money. Needing a drink so badly, I went into the bathroom and tried to open a bottle of after-shave lotion. My hands were trembling so violently that I couldn't get the plastic cap off. So I broke the neck of the bottle and drank what was left. The lotion should have killed me, but the death I desired never came.

One evening I wandered into Mom's house during a prayer meeting and shocked all the ladies by mocking God in front of them. I even began threatening Mom — something I had never done before. She didn't know when I might get violent, so if I was sleeping in her house, Mom would go to bed with an open Bible lying on her chest.

By this time Brinda was so upset that she went to Mom's doctor. I had become so filled with rage that even she was afraid of me. I was really mean to her. The doctor said, "Brinda, the best thing you can do is leave this guy. He's an animal! Just forget him! Act as if he's died, and then start a new life for yourself." And he prescribed a bottle of tranquilizers for her.

A few days later I was outside, shooting target practice with my gun. Then I came in and began drinking some more. I was raving around the apartment, cursing Brinda as if she were responsible for the terrible depression I was experiencing that day. Brinda looked at me with such love, fear and hate all mixed together! She decided she couldn't live *with* me and couldn't live *without* me. So she quietly went into the bathroom and swallowed the entire bottle (about forty pills) of Valium. Brinda walked out and told me that she was committing suicide: she couldn't stand living with me any longer.

I just shrugged my shoulders: "Well, that's your thing!" And I wandered into the bedroom. A few minutes later I walked out and noticed that Brinda appeared to be unconscious. As foggy as my mind was, I finally realized that I should do something. I phoned Mom at work: "Mom, Brinda's committed suicide, I guess. She took a bunch of Valium."

Mom jumped in her car and rushed to our apartment. Somehow she got Brinda in the car and took her to the hospital, where they began to pump her stomach. Mom loved that little girl!

I was alone. "Brinda's dead! I've messed up everybody's life I ever touched!" I sat there pondering the situation for awhile.

"Why am I doing all this thinking?" And I drank some more. But I couldn't stop thinking!

I looked at my gun, sitting on the table. "There's nothing left; why not?"

I picked up the gun and put a magazine in it. I cocked it, opened my mouth, stuck the gun down my throat and pulled the trigger.

Click!

No explosion! Nothing but a click! I took the bullet out. There was an indentation on the shell where the hammer had struck it. Yet it hadn't fired! I cursed it and loaded the pistol again.

I opened my mouth and pulled the trigger.

Click!

I slammed the gun against the wall, then looked at the ceiling and cursed God! "I hate you, God! You won't even let me die! I don't understand what you want of me! Just let me die!" Then I gathered up some more pills and washed them down with the rest of my liquor.

Several hours later Brinda and Mom walked in. I couldn't believe it: "I thought you were dead!"

Mom was excited: "David! God worked another miracle! Those pills were in her stomach for nearly an hour, but when the doctor pumped her stomach, not one of them had dissolved!"

"What," I thought, "does this God want of me? Why is everybody else so excited about these miracles, and I'm so miserable? I hate all this talk about miracles! I can't stand to live, and He won't let me die! Why is He picking on *me*?"

Chapter 9

One of Us Had to Die

It had been almost two years since Jesus had lengthened my leg. Those should have been happy years, but it was the most miserable period of my miserable life. The "cocktails" of drugs I was shooting in my arms would leave me mindless for days at a time. Then I'd be broke again and have to figure how to rob someone. I was sick all the time. My liver was swollen and hard; my kidneys wouldn't function properly; the yellowish color of my skin was becoming more prominent each month.

One day I was drinking with a kid who complained that he had been fired from his waiter's job at the country club. Then he started telling about a big poker game that was scheduled there. "Every year around Labor Day a bunch of doctors lock themselves in the country club, and play poker all weekend. Last year, while I was serving drinks, I saw at least a hundred thousand dollars on that table!"

Suddenly I got interested. I called for Snake and several other guys, and they walked over to listen to this kid's story. We'd never pulled a big job like this before, but it sounded awfully good. The former waiter described the layout of the building in great detail. I planned carefully, assigning one guy to disconnect the burglar alarm, others to do different jobs. On Saturday we would rob a sporting goods store to get some shotguns, and then hit the poker game early Sunday morning.

Somebody asked, "What do we do if one of the doctors gives us some trouble?"

Snake answered confidently, "Don't worry. That'll never happen. When we first go in there, I'm going to *kill* one of them! That'll scare the rest, and they won't cause any problems."

I wondered about that. I don't think I could have killed a man without provocation, but it didn't seem to bother Snake at all.

We had the plans all set to rob the doctors' poker game at the country club early Sunday morning. But by Wednesday evening I was feeling so sick, I didn't know if I would live until Sunday. So Brinda and I went to Mom's house. Mom could see how sick I was, so she led me into a bedroom where I lay down. "David, why don't you ask Jesus to help you?"

"Mom! I'm so sick of hearing about Jesus! I don't want to hear about Him anymore! He's been driving me crazy for the last two years!"

"David, please ask Jesus to help you!"

"Mom, if you don't quit talking about Jesus, I'm going to hurt you!"

But she wouldn't quit. Suddenly, I jumped up from the bed and hit her in the face, knocking her to the floor and breaking her glasses. She got up slowly and said, "David, I guess you're just going to have to kill me, because I'm not leaving this room until you ask Jesus to help you!"

"Mom! Don't you know I *will* kill you if you don't shut up and get out of here?"

She answered quietly, "Then you're going to have to kill me."

I didn't know how to deal with Mom's boldness, so I lay there a few minutes and thought about it. Finally I asked, "Well, all right! How do I do it?"

"Just say 'Jesus, help me!'"

I started to say it, but my mouth was suddenly slammed shut! I couldn't say "Jesus"! Something seemed to have me by the throat, and I couldn't talk! Within a few moments I became violently ill.

Mom told Brinda to call Tim. He said he wouldn't come over. Brinda pleaded.

Tim exploded, "I'm tired of his lies! I've had it!"

"But your mother wants you to come!"

"Brinda, there's no use! Neither one of you is ready! And even if David got straightened out, you'd still have to get yourself straightened out, too!"

Brinda wouldn't give up. Finally, Tim sighed, "Oh, all right! I'll come over and listen to the same baloney one more time!" Claudia came along, and she spent the evening in Mom's living room talking with Brinda.

Tim walked into the bedroom, and I went wild! Jumping from the bed, I grabbed him by the shirt and lifted him off the floor! I slammed him against the wall and shouted, in a voice that was not mine, "I hate you! I'm going to kill you!" Tim was a husky six-footer, weighing about 230 pounds, and my body was so wasted that I weighed barely half that much! Suddenly, I had superhuman strength, and a supernatural voice to match!

I let Tim go, and fell back on the bed. Tim hurried into another room, his shirt torn and his face bleeding. He was trembling, realizing that he had just confronted Satan himself. Tim got on his knees and prayed, "Jesus, forgive me for my attitude! Help me to help my brother."

When Tim returned to the bedroom, I jumped up to hit him. But he pointed his finger at me and shouted, "Satan! I command you in the name of the Lord Jesus to come out of David!"

I couldn't move! I tried to kill Tim, but I couldn't even touch him! I fell over on the bed — helpless! I'd always laughed when Christians had told me I was full of demons. But suddenly I thought maybe it was true! I was trembling violently! Where had all that strength come from? And that voice?

Tim repeated again and again, "David! Call on Jesus! Ask Jesus to set you free!"

I tried; but each time a force would clamp my mouth shut and try to choke me. I could not say "Jesus"! Mom and Tim prayed and prayed. I lay there for perhaps two hours. It seemed to be a stalemate.

Then Mom and Tim began naming individual demons, commanding them to come out in the name of Jesus Christ. Demons of hatred and murder, perversion, lust, lying, alcoholism and many others. I could feel the sensation of each one leaving. I was growing weaker by the hour, and the pain in my body was intense.

Several times I grabbed my brother's hand and pleaded, "Tim! Whatever you're doing, don't give up! Please don't give up!"

A few minutes later I'd be cursing Tim again in that strange voice. And I still couldn't say the name of Jesus!

Tim knew he had the victory though, and he and Mom continued urging me to call on Jesus. After hours of prayer and deliverance, I tried again, and finally the Name came out: "Jesus! Jesus, help me!"

Instantly I was free! I knew it! The last demon was gone! We hugged each other and laughed and cried. Then we prayed some more.

But I had deceived Tim so many times that he thought he should verify my experience. He called several of his minister-friends. They graciously got out of bed in the middle of the night and came to Mom's house. They asked questions, and I answered. After prayer and conversation until well into the night, they all agreed that I was free. I was thrilled to be able to ask Jesus Christ to become the Lord of my life!

I looked at Brinda and Claudia, and they were

all aglow. Brinda announced with joy that she had just accepted Jesus, too!

It was September 6, 1972. I was thirty-one years old when God finally answered Mom's prayers. My body was so sick and so weak, I could hardly get off the living room couch, but now I knew my sins were forgiven and I had eternal life! As evil as I had been, I was totally aware that God had forgiven all my sins. *All* of them! Now I knew exactly what they were talking about when Christians said they were "born again"!

Sixteen years of warfare between Mom and me ended. I had always known that one of us would have to die, and David Kelton died that night. A new man was born from the dead!

Tim and Claudia left happy, and Mom walked out to the car with them, leaving only Brinda and me in the house. I was so weak and trembling that I told Brinda, "I've got a bottle of wine hidden in that closet. I've got to have a drink! Get it for me!" Brinda obediently searched for it and brought the wine bottle to me. With shaking hands I ripped the top off and started to take a drink. But before I got it to my lips, I stopped. "No! I'm a Christian now! I don't need this stuff anymore! Brinda! Pour this garbage down the drain!"

Mom walked back into the house to see

Brinda pouring out the wine. It seemed to be the final confirmation. Mom could see for herself that alcohol had not been my problem: she had been dealing with the devil, just as the evangelist had told her.

In spite of the nervousness, I fell into a deep sleep on the couch. Brinda was beginning a new job that morning, and she went to work with very little rest, yet she was alert and peaceful all day.

Awaking alone hours later, I felt quite refreshed and very much at peace within myself. I also felt a strange sensation of wanting a bath. So I bathed, shaved and put on clean clothes, then fell back on the couch exhausted. When they arrived home, Mom and Brinda were thrilled to see see me all cleaned up. I ate my first meal in two weeks, then slept most of the time until Sunday — the first peaceful sleep since I was fifteen years old! Every waking moment I marveled at the total freedom from withdrawal. The *peace* I felt was so satisfying! I had gone through a hell during withdrawal at Hope Harbor in Greensboro. This time it was all peaceful and pleasant.

I was still sick in my body: my liver was swollen and my skin yellow, my kidneys were in terrible condition, I was weak and trembling, I was still chain-smoking cigarettes, and my language was still embarrassing to Mom — but I knew I was a Christian! I realized that Jesus wanted to love me, instead of torment me. He was now my Friend!

That Sunday morning we all went to Tim's church. I could feel the stares of many people I had hurt, and I was truly embarrassed for the first time since I had been a boy. I had almost forgotten what embarrassment felt like. Everybody wondered why I was in church. But I was determined that, for the first time in my adult life, I was going to face reality. At the appropriate moment, I gathered my courage and stood up. Stumbling through my testimony, I shared what Jesus had done for me three days earlier. Nearly all of them had that "Well, we'll see!" look on their faces.

All, that is, except David Rowell. This ex-hippie put his arm around me and began to talk about my salvation experience. David had come with the group of ministers who verified my deliverance the previous Wednesday night, and he had immediately observed the spectacular change in me. David suggested that he move into Mom's house to help me. Mom was delighted to have him.

David taught me for hours on end, night after night. He'd tell me a simple truth about Jesus, but I couldn't remember it long enough to repeat it back to him. The drugs and alcohol had so damaged my brain that very little was registering. I could barely read and write, but David was patient, and I truly wanted to learn. Repeating a simple biblical fact over and over, David would literally saturate my burned-out brain with the Word of God. God was faithful as He slowly restored my mind. David Rowell lived with us for six weeks, until he felt his work was completed. Then he quietly moved out. I could now read the Bible for myself.

Terry Sue and her husband also loved me that first Sunday. They even invited me to come to work on Monday. So weak that I could hardly pick up a hammer, they patiently encouraged me as my strength slowly returned. The other workmen were watching in disbelief because most of them had known me. Yet, I was so different that a few weeks later they began calling me "Preacher." My hard, swollen abdomen began softening, and God healed it within days. The ugly yellow color of my skin was another matter; it started to fade almost imperceptibly as my kidneys slowly improved. God was gently healing me — healing irreversible physical damage.

Through the years the Lord had obviously taught Mom some wonderful things. She didn't recoil at my profanity, but trusted the Holy Spirit to teach me a new language. She never protested as I kept the house blue with cigarette smoke. Mom gave all of those problems to Jesus.

Another miracle happened so quietly that I almost missed it. One day Mom told Brinda to do something, and Brinda quietly replied, "Yes, ma'am." I could hardly believe my ears! As I pondered Brinda's response, the full reality struck me. She doesn't argue any more!

Later Brinda heard a teaching on Ephesians 5: "Wives, be subject to your husbands . . ." Ever since, Brinda has been totally submissive to my leadership. Indeed, other Christians are utterly astonished at her obedience. *God* transformed Brinda into a lady and a wife. She is contented and happy, and yet has some quite effective ways of changing my mind when she knows I'm about to make a mistake.

As an alcoholic, I had always been fearful of not having a drink when I needed it. Two years earlier I had been stuck in Mom's house without alcohol for weeks after the wreck, so I had to make sure it wouldn't happen again. During that time, therefore, I had hidden "emergency" money and booze around Mom's house, but couldn't recall where they were. So Mom, Brinda and I initiated what must have looked like an Easter egg hunt. Even many months later we'd enjoy a good laugh as a bottle of wine would be found in the corner of a closet, or a handful of bills would appear in the bottom of a drawer.

Brinda and I shared a fear which we didn't repeat to anyone else. We had heard of numerous sinners, including my sister Marquita's ophthalmologist, who had accepted Jesus Christ, then died soon afterward. Therefore, we both expected to die at any time. Assuming that God wanted only to save us from hell and get us to heaven, we were literally anticipating death daily. We could have been set free if we had only asked for prayer, but we were too embarrassed to say anything about it. Our one consolation was that we knew that God had granted us eternal life, and we would die with assurance. We'd awake each new morning, thankful for God's gift, never realizing that Satan was the author of that fear of death.

Actually, I figured the guys who were to be involved in the Sunday holdup at the country club would kill me. I had been planning the whole operation, and they must have felt betrayed after I disappeared, causing the holdup to be cancelled. Fully expecting to look up into a gun barrel some day, I thought it would be Snake who would shoot me. Knowing what I had been like, I had every reason to fear Snake's anger. I waited daily for many weeks, wondering when it was going to happen. I never returned to the Beef 'n Rib again.

Everyone advised me to stay away from the Trade Street section of Charlotte; they were afraid I might be killed if I went back there — even to talk about the Lord.

Otherwise, things went well for several weeks. Then one night, while lying in bed, I began sensing that insatiable craving for some drugs. Within minutes my body was screaming for drugs! That night I had the fight of my life. I walked the floor until dawn, carrying my Bible, trying to read a sentence whenever I could. Somehow, I knew I'd been given my last chance, and I wasn't going to lose it. The desire finally left with the daylight, but I was severely shaken, knowing that it would happen again that night. Each time would get worse, and I knew there was no way I could continue to resist that terrible craving.

I went to work without sleep — angry at God. "Lord! I don't understand this! You know I can't handle this torment much longer!" All day I worked with a sullen attitude. Before quitting time I resolved that when the desire for drugs got too strong for me, I was just going to give in. "So *there*, God! If that's all the power You've got, I'll just go back to the pills!"

I dreaded to see nighttime approach. It was Thursday — Prayer Meeting night — so I went to church, seating myself defiantly in the rear. At the close of the service, Tim invited those who wanted prayer to come to the front of the church. "That's for me!" I thought, and I started forward. But so did everyone else! And they all got there first!

Now I was really angry at God! "Listen, God! *I'm* the one who needs prayer! Don't You care about me?"

Finally, Tim finished praying for all the others. He noticed me to one side, away from the rest of the congregation, pouting. Tim sensed what was in my heart as soon as he looked at me. He prayed silently, "Lord, David has felt Satan's power so long; let him feel Your power this one time!"

As he had done for all the others, Tim put a little anointing oil on his finger and moved toward me, raising his hand to place it on my forehead. He was within inches of my head when suddenly an enormous charge of electricity jolted me! Tim was knocked backward; I was catapulted in the other direction, and slammed into the wall ten feet away! I fell forward on my face and lay motionless on the floor.

The congregation quickly gathered around me. When they heard me praying in tongues, they knew I was all right. Several knelt and laid their hands on me as everyone was praying joyously. All their suspicions about me vanished in that moment.

An hour later I was still on the floor, praying in tongues — totally oblivious to what was going on. I was not unconscious, yet I cannot remember anything about those hours. Folks slowly began going home, aglow with excitement.

About eleven p.m. a man named Henry Polk said, "Tim, you need to get home. I'll stay with David and make sure he's okay." I was still praying in tongues.

Three hours passed, and I made no signs of reviving. Henry continued to sit on the front pew, watching me and praying for me. At some time after midnight, I opened my eyes. Looking up to see Henry, I asked, "What happened?"

"David, God just baptized you in the Holy Spirit. Now you're filled with His power. You have been praying in tongues for more than three hours!"

I was mystified. I could hardly believe that God would actually fill someone like me with His Holy Spirit! But I felt good. In fact, as I stood up, I began to feel a joy, an exhilaration. That night I slept like a baby.

In the years since, I have never once had another desire for drugs of any sort. There has never been a craving for liquor, either. I am *different* from Alcoholics Anonymous: I am no longer an alcoholic! God set me free from that demon when He filled me with His Holy Spirit — His personal Power dwelling within me. I learned very quickly that God is far more powerful than Satan.

Now I was really free! I felt a confidence in Jesus Christ that I hadn't known before. He was more real and personal than ever. Sitting down to read the Bible at every opportunity, I was feeding on the scripture like a starving man. My intellectual nature had always been to question everything I read, but I heard a voice within me, saying, "Believe the Bible as you read it; don't try to understand everything before you believe." So I read as a trusting child, and discovered to my delight that I began understanding the Bible as I was reading it.

But Mom and Tim were puzzled about one thing: How could I be filled with the Holy Spirit and still smoke those dirty cigarettes? I began wondering too after they discussed it with me. One day, when I was alone in Mom's house, I felt a strange sensation. I seemed to be aware that I would never smoke another cigarette. Walking around the house, I gathered up all the ashtrays and all the cigarettes, and threw them out. And indeed, I have never smoked since. Again, no struggle or withdrawal, only the power of God.

Chapter 10

Opening Doors

Several days later Tim made a provocative statement: "David, you've been saved and filled with the Holy Spirit. You can't just sit around reading the Bible all the time. You've got to get out and do something for the Lord!"

"Like what?"

"Well, we have a new television ministry called the PTL Club. It includes a telephone counseling service. Maybe you can do some volunteer carpenter work for us." So that Saturday I walked into the counseling room to see if I could make some desks for the counselors. There I saw one man — Sandy Wheeler — with a telephone in each hand and all the other telephones ringing.

When he saw me, Sandy yelled, "Answer a phone!"

I held up my hands helplessly.

"Answer a phone!" Sandy demanded.

"You don't understand," I tried to explain. "I don't know anything . . ."

"Answer a phone!" Sandy was determined.

So I cautiously walked up to one of the telephones. Sandy was talking rapidly into one telephone while holding the other away from his mouth, nodding forcefully to me and glaring at the telephone in front of me. It continued to ring insistently.

Timidly I picked it up. "Hello?"

"I'm going to kill myself!" announced a woman's voice.

"Oh, no!" I sighed. "Why did I answer the telephone?"

I looked helplessly toward Sandy, but he was already deeply involved in his two counseling calls. "What can I say to this woman? I hardly know Matthew from Mark!"

I stammered for a moment, then began to tell her the only spiritual thing I knew — my testimony of what Jesus had done for me. Not listening to me, she kept on talking about her problems and the desperation she felt. I got louder, and she got louder. With irritation in my voice, I told her to "shut up!" Finally, she quit talking and began to listen. After I told her everything the Lord had done for me, she asked if I thought He would do the same for her. I suggested that He would, and she accepted Jesus Christ as her Lord — right over the telephone!

I *floated* out of that counseling center! The next day I was right back. Day after day I counseled there, listening to miracles occur over the telephones. It was thrilling! Wild horses couldn't have kept me away. Each day I'd finish my work, and then head for the television counseling center.

I loved the peace of God that I felt in my heart. I could now lie down and go to sleep peacefully for the first time in many years. I tried to think back to when that restlessness all started. The Army psychiatrist decided that I had been a hyperactive child, but he was not correct. That deep anxiety began during my teen years — *after* I made the decision that there was no God! That was it! My professed atheism — when I knew better — brought a conviction of sin in my heart that only Jesus could correct. All my reading of occult books only made the anxiety worse.

I had often wondered about my great-grandfather's family — how he could have been a wealthy doctor, his son have a lesser position, his grandson — my father — become a common laborer, and I develop into a criminal. It was four generations of *atheism* that did it — a continual degrading with each successive generation! The Second Commandment describes it well: "I the Lord your God am a jealous God, visiting the iniquity of the fathers upon the children to the third and fourth generation of those who hate Me . . ." (Exodus 20:5). Only the prayers of Mom, Tim, Terry Sue and countless others changed that awful judgment upon my life.

And all those times when I was spared Army court martial and jail sentences and accidental death and suicide! I had always thought I was lucky. That was *not luck*! God was watching over me! I had been chosen to *live*!

Now Brinda and I were growing and maturing by leaps and bounds. Our Christian family gave us audio tapes of sermons by well-known Christian teachers. As we sensed our faith being built up, the tapes gave us a desire to attend a Christian conference. Hearing about a Morris Cerullo conference in San Diego, Brinda and I asked God to provide the money for us to attend. Little by little He did, and we flew to San Diego for a spiritual feast during Christmas week. After one of the Cerullo services, I found myself planning in my mind for the future. Realizing with a start that I no longer expected to die, I told Brinda that God had just set me free. Brinda bubbled as she perceived that God had set her free from the fear of death, too! Both of us at the same time! We returned home to Charlotte, delivered from that bondage.

The fledgling PTL television ministry — all run by volunteers — was providing a real service to the Charlotte community. After we returned from San Diego, Brinda was asked to become one of the PTL Club's first paid employees. Brinda quit her restaurant job, and found herself assigned to an adding machine and a typewriter — never having operated either of them! Within a year Brinda was competent on the typewriter and — literally — a genius on the adding machine. She learned to maintain — with both speed and accuracy — as many as seven adding machines at once. This skill was essential for telethons.

Tim was co-host of the PTL Club, but everyone realized that the program needed someone with that distinct calling to be on camera every day. Jim Bakker was asked by the Board of Directors to come from California in the spring, and the PTL Club took off like a skyrocket!

Jim Bakker began holding rallies around the Greater Charlotte area, and I volunteered to be an usher. Jim learned very quickly to trust me, giving me increasing responsibilities. The PTL Club

123

nearly went bankrupt during the first growing year, so the Lord provided large offerings at several of these rallies. After one service, somebody had a sizable offering that needed to be deposited in the bank quickly. He asked Jim Bakker what should be done with the money, and Jim said, "Give it to David Kelton to take back to Charlotte. He can be trusted."

"But Jim, you don't know Kelton's track record! He's been in and out of jail!"

"Give the money to him! He can be trusted." Jim's response got back to me. After hearing that, I think I might have given my life for him.

Brinda had been experiencing some painful physical problems from the time she went to work for the PTL Club. She finally went to the doctor and was referred to a specialist. His tests confirmed that she had cancer! Brinda and I both had the most unusual responses to this horrible news: we were not troubled in the least! The Lord had so wonderfully delivered us from the fear of death during the previous Christmas season that we were utterly unshaken. Each of us knew everything would be all right. So we did nothing beyond committing the problem to God. The specialist wanted to perform surgery immediately, but agreed to wait until after the completion of the

PTL telethon the following Wednesday. He prescribed medicine for the pain, but Brinda refused to have the prescription filled. She even went back to her adding machines without telling anyone other than Mom, Tim and Claudia, who were praying for her. We both felt a little guilty that we weren't worried, as people normally expect.

The PTL telethon was exciting, and I was made volunteer captain of the counseling phones. On Saturday night I left the telethon to teach my regular Bible study. (Would you believe I was already teaching a Bible study? And a well-attended session at that!) I was standing in front of perhaps fifty college-age young people, when suddenly I was aware that Brinda was healed of cancer! That wonderful bit of knowledge was so interruptive to the flow of my teaching that I couldn't consider it at the moment.

However, at the PTL Club Jim Bakker abruptly broke into his fundraising on television to announce, "God has just healed one of our viewers of cancer!"

"No . . . ," Jim added thoughtfully, "it's in the studio audience."

"No, it's not!" he spoke emphatically. "It's . . . it's . . . one of our employees! . . . That's right!" Jim swung his arm around and pointed toward the adding machines: "It's *you*, Brinda!" Jim knew nothing of the doctor's diagnosis!

Brinda could hardly wait for me to pick her up after my Bible study class. "Guess what happened to me!" she bubbled.

"God healed you!"

"How did you know?"

"He told me during my Bible study!"

And she was indeed healed! Brinda returned to the surgeon, requesting that he repeat his tests. It seemed like a waste of time and money, but he made the tests again. Brinda thoroughly enjoyed witnessing about Jesus to her astonished doctor! She remains healed to this day!

John Stephenson at Hope Harbor in Greensboro heard about my salvation, so he invited me to share my testimony during a Sunday morning service. *Eleven* of those alcoholics accepted Jesus that morning! I could understand these men and their problems, and they all knew it. Returning to Charlotte with such joy and excitement in my heart, I began pondering a new idea — perhaps I should go to Bible college and study to be a minister!

For days I thought about Bible college. After

all, I loved to pray on the telephone at the PTL Club, and God had blessed my ministry at Hope Harbor. Then one night I couldn't sleep. A thought was coming into my mind all night: I should work for the PTL Club. "But that's ridiculous! I don't know anything about television." I went to work without sleep, but all day long the thought was reappearing in my mind. That night I collapsed into bed, utterly exhausted. Still my eyes would not stay shut. I tossed and turned, trying to forget the nagging thought that I should work for the PTL Club. "I can't just walk in there and tell them to hire me!" I didn't get a wink of sleep that night either.

Finally I decided to settle the matter; I had to have some sleep. About dawn of the second sleepless night, I got out of bed and drove to the PTL Club. Of course, no one would be there at that hour, so the trip seemed a waste of time. As I parked my car, I noticed a light in the office. There was Sandy Wheeler, already at work! I felt as if the Lord was closing walls around me.

I sat in the car for some time, arguing with God. "But what am I going to tell Sandy, Lord?" No answer.

At last I gathered my courage and tiptoed in. "Hi, Sandy."

"Well, good morning, David. What brings you here so early?"

"Oh, I couldn't sleep, and I need to talk to you before I go to work this morning."

"What do you want?" Sandy was all business.

"Well, this may sound silly, but God keeps telling me that I'm supposed to go to work for PTL."

"What would you be able to do?" Sandy asked soberly.

"I know I'm not a trained minister, but perhaps I could be in charge of the telephone counselors."

"David, you know we have no money to hire *anybody* else. But I have a strange feeling that God *does* want you here. We're having a Board of Directors meeting this morning — that's why I'm here so early, getting these papers together — I'll bring it up to them."

I walked out and went to work — still feeling silly, yet relieved of that continual urging in my spirit. When I arrived home that evening, Sandy called to tell me that the Board agreed. They didn't know where they'd find the money, or even what I would be doing, but all of them knew that God wanted me there full-time. And I slept peacefully all night.

Chapter 11

Television

In the morning I told Terry Sue's husband that I felt God was calling me to the PTL Club, and gave him two weeks notice. He was as excited as I was! Telling me to complete the job I was working on, he released me immediately — with the two weeks' pay anyhow! Working on Saturday, I finished the last of the job so I could begin at PTL on Monday.

Sandy announced as soon as I arrived on Monday morning that I would be working in television. "But, I thought . . . " Sandy would not listen to my protests. "But the telephones . . ." No, I would report to Sam Orender, the director of the live PTL Club program.

Sam was visibly upset. "You don't know anything about television?" Well, here! Take this broom and sweep the studio." Some time later, Sam came back to tell me I'd be running camera for the show that morning.

"Camera? You're kidding!"

"Nope! The rest of the crew left for a telethon in Paducah. Sandy won't run camera for me; he says you're it."

"But what do I do?"

Sam gave me a few quick instructions and handed me the earphones. Actually, we had only one trained cameraman in the studio. He ran camera three, the one requiring the most skill. Sam locked down camera two to get a wide shot of everybody on the set, and put me on camera one, "the training camera." All I had to do was focus the camera and keep it on Jim Bakker. I was the oldest employee in the studio, yet I knew the least about television.

The program started and I was a nervous wreck. Sam's voice boomed in the earphone: "Camera one, truck left!"

"Hey! Camera one! That's you, Kelton!" I jumped.

"Camera one, pan left!" Sam's voice was rising in volume. I moved the handles on the camera to the left.

"Left! Camera one! Pan *left*!" Suddenly I realized that if I moved the handles *left*, the picture moved in the opposite direction. Quickly I turned the other way.

"Camera one! You're cutting off the top of Jim's head! Get the picture up!" Sam Orender was almost beside himself as he envisioned the program being carried on stations across the country.

"Camera one! When Jim bends over, keep him in the picture!" Sam was screaming!

"No! Camera one! You're cutting off the top of his head again!" And so it went — for two horribly long hours! Sam must have wanted to hit me over the head with a baseball bat. Actually, Sam was very kind and helpful to me; he was merely exasperated with the situation.

Following the program that afternoon, I experimented with the camera, and the next day I did a little better. On Wednesday our only experienced cameraman was also sent to Paducah for the telethon, and I had to run camera three — the most difficult of all! We found a volunteer to run camera one. Then the telethon crew needed the audio man in Paducah, so poor Sam Orender had to direct and run audio, too — a nearly impossible task. When the Friday morning program ended, all of us who remained in Charlotte jumped in a station wagon and headed for Paducah. And I loved every minute of it!

A year had passed since my salvation. The yellowish cast to my skin was almost gone, but I still was having trouble with my left leg. Actually, all the injuries from the car accident were now healed, but these problems in my leg were of earlier origin. My left knee had been injured and re-injured in high school football and weight-lifting, and my ankle had been broken in the Army. Neither one was totally healed, so I had learned even as a teenager to live with the pain that was always there. If I would be on my feet running camera for a long time, my ankle would swell and bleed, even to the point of filling my shoe with blood. Occasionally, the left knee would buckle without warning, and I would tumble to the floor, then get back up in spite of the pain and work as if nothing had happened. Because of these injuries, I could still go up stairs only one at a time. But I loved the Christian television ministry so much that the continuing pain was shoved into the background.

One day Sam Orender, who also did the lighting for the PTL Club studio, developed Bell's palsy. Because his face was drawn to one side, Sam was unable to do the lighting. Suddenly I was the studio lighting man — and I had barely learned how to run camera! But studio lighting came naturally to me, and to this day that complex art is one of my special interests.

The PTL Club was being carried on a rapidly

increasing number of television stations, so more and more I found myself being assigned to telethon crews in cities across the nation. While running camera for a telethon in Columbia, South Carolina, my left ankle became terribly swollen, painful and bleeding after hours on camera. I simply *had* to get off that leg. The director let me take a break, so I rested on the edge of the music set. Seeing me sitting there, Jim Bakker shouted, "David Kelton! Come here!"

I hobbled out in front of the cameras, where Jim put his arm around me and spent forty-five minutes telling my testimony. Then he invited viewers to call in and accept Jesus as Lord. *Six hundred people* telephoned the studio that day to make that all-important decision! Certainly, hundreds more could not get their calls through — and Columbia is one of the nation's smaller television markets! I think it was a record day at the PTL Club for salvations. I knew then that my testimony was not mine alone — it was God's — and I should share it whenever I was asked.

The entire time Jim Bakker was telling my story, he had a bear hug around my neck. I wanted to sit down so badly! When Jim finally let me go, I sat down and examined my left ankle. To my surprise the swelling was almost gone and the bleeding stopped! The ankle has never bled since that day, and the swelling was greatly reduced!

The PTL Club had a large portable telethon set which we took to each affiliate TV station twice a year. The telethon set was so bulky that a rented tractor-trailor was required to transport it. Then we needed three days to assemble it in Chattanooga or San Francisco or Worcester. All this effort challenged me. I spent many hours of my spare time — of which we had very little, because we worked long days on the road — figuring out a more compact telethon set. After some tinkering, I designed and built a set that could be carried in a van and assembled in five hours.

Jim Bakker was impressed, and he encouraged me to proceed further. I continued to refine the concept, until I designed and built a telethon set that could actually be folded into cases and taken with us on commercial airliners. Already Jim Bakker knew he could trust me, so he insisted that I be given further responsibilities. I was promoted to "Propmaster." As such, I had to build all the sets for the PTL Club — and the job was becoming increasingly complex.

As the network grew, highly-skilled people across the nation were applying for employment at PTL. Many felt genuinely called by God, while others were merely sick of the hassles in commercial television. For whatever reasons they came, I inherited two extremely competent men in my prop department — Bill Healy and Lewis Sustar. Bill had an executive background in addition to all the skills and experience needed for constructing — literally — anything. Lewis was so talented in carpentry that he could build anything made of wood. I may have been their boss, but both were older and far more experienced.

With each passing week, I felt the growing intimidation of supervising two men more capable than I. Finally, I couldn't stand it any longer. That night I dropped to my knees and prayed, "Lord, You know I love this job. But Bill is a better supervisor than I am, and both Bill and Lewis know more about the work than I do. I give the job of Propmaster to You. If You want Bill to have my position, it's okay with me."

The very next morning Dale Hill, PTL's General Manager, called me into his office. "David, we've decided to move you out of that job."

I stared at Dale. I'd never heard of a "prayer of relinquishment" being answered so quickly! "All right, Lord," I thought, "I'll accept a demotion."

Dale went on. "We are making Lewis Sustar the Propmaster."

Lewis? In my mind I had picked Bell Healy! But I didn't dispute the decision; they were both good men. I would accept working under Lewis if that was what God wanted of me.

Dale smiled slightly. "We are promoting you to Production Manager!"

Production Manager! With the responsibility of supervising more than twenty-five employees? Me? I was in a state of shock! After I went home, I was praying and thanking God. I knew in my heart that without the prayer of relinquishment the night before, I never would have been promoted. As I continued thanking God, He showed me a vision. In this vision *sand* was pouring into my hands, but as I closed my hands to grasp it, all the sand leaked out around my fingers. When I held my hands open, the sand piled up freely on my open palms. The Lord spoke in my heart, "I can bless you only as you release what you have!" It was quite a lesson!

I thoroughly enjoyed being Production Manager. Feeling challenged intellectually for the first time in many years, the job forced me to research and learn. All of us were unprepared for the miracle growth of the PTL Club, and it was causing everyone to make serious mistakes. I was determined to make as few mistakes as possible. I experimented with new ideas; I was fair with all of my employees; and we developed a smoothly-operating department. It was fun!

Brinda and I were so busy — working unbelievably long hours — and experiencing so much true enjoyment of life that we scarcely thought of our sordid past years. Yet one broken relationship still grieved us, especially Brinda. Her parents would have nothing to do with her!

Even Brinda's brother and three sisters remembered her as an incorrigible child: the more she was beaten, the more rebellious she became. I had seen several startling examples of her violent temper when I had abused her. After Brinda had begun living with me, she wrote a letter to her parents. The letter was returned, torn apart, inside another envelope which said, "We don't have a daughter by that name!" Every letter after the first one had come back unopened, saying, "Return to sender." Brinda's heart would be broken each time. After we accepted Jesus, Brinda wrote her parents several times, explaining how Jesus had changed her. But the letters were always sent back unopened, with those crushing words: "Return to sender."

Several years later Brinda and I were in a motel room in Traverse City, Michigan, where the PTL Club was having a telethon. The telephone rang, and Brinda answered it. Her mother's voice said, very coldly, "Brinda, pray for your father; he has blood clots in his lung, and the doctor doesn't think he'll make it."

Brinda tried to talk, but the tears welled up, and I had to take the telephone from her. The brief conversation was confusing. We thought her mother would phone again with a progress report, but her mother was assuming that Brinda would call in a few days. Brinda was in a state of shock after I hung up the telephone. Eleven cruel years had passed without contact. How many things she wished she had said on the telephone! How many questions she wished she had asked! But her mother's coolness made us hesitant to phone them.

Brinda and I wondered about her father's condition for another full year of silence. Finally her mother called again, and this time Brinda was prepared. Her dad was okay. She learned that her parents had known all about us through some friends in Charlotte. That day Brinda's mother invited us to visit them in Georgia. It was a genuine miracle in response to agonizing prayer. Brinda excitedly agreed that we'd come for Thanksgiving.

"David, what should I say? How should I act? How do I deal with the rejection? Do you think they'll be nice to me?" Brinda was more nervous than I'd ever seen her.

"I think you should treat them as if they were the best parents in the whole world."

"But David! How can I do that? You know how they treated me."

"Brinda," I countered, "in Jesus' power you can do it."

Brinda was so nervous as we drove to Savannah for Thanksgiving. Her dad began to cry the moment he saw Brinda; the tears flowed freely in a bittersweet reunion. Except for Brinda's brother, who lives in Alaska, everyone was there for Thanksgiving. And the "black sheep" of the family did it! Brinda loved them all. Later she privately called her parents long distance, and they both accepted Jesus Christ on the telephone!

Brinda was ecstatic! Jesus gave her the grace to love her parents, and they responded to that love. They were astonished at the dramatic change in Brinda. Her parents remembered only an arguing, vile-mouthed, vengeful teenager, but at Thanksgiving they had seen a gentle, loving daughter. Jesus has so transformed Brinda's parents also that I have difficulty imagining them as having mistreated their active, difficult child. We love to visit them during vacations. Several years ago we prayed again for her dad when he appeared to be dying, and God healed him once more.

After being promoted to Production Manager, I had to remain in Charlotte most of the time. More opportunities for Bible studies arose. Indeed, I had invitations to teach three weekly sessions in communities nearby. Tim asked me to become his assistant pastor and — what a delight! — I found myself preaching and teaching, exactly as I had prayed several years before! Jim Bakker asked me to be the Bible teacher at Heritage Village Church each Wednesday afternoon, and later I taught on Sunday afternoons at the new campground. God gave me all the preaching and teaching I could handle!

I received an invitation to preach an entire week's revival for a convocation of several black congregations near Charlotte. While preaching one of those evenings, I looked down at the front row, and there was a man who looked like . . . No! It couldn't be! That guy looks like *Snake*! It *is* Snake! I guess this is it! He's come to kill me! And I preached that night as if that would be my last sermon!

Every once in a while I'd sneak a look at

Snake in the front row, and each time he'd be grinning at me. He didn't appear the way he used to. And I wondered. By the end of my message I decided that something good must have happened to Snake. I ran down the steps and we threw our arms around each other! "You're saved!"

"Praise the Lord! You are, too!"

"But, Snake!" I demanded. "Where have you been? I haven't seen you at all!"

"You mean, 'Where have *you* been?'" Snake protested. "*I've* been down on Trade Street, passing out tracts and talking to everybody about the Lord!"

"Well, all my friends warned me never to go back there. In fact, I was afraid you were going to kill me if you saw me!"

"Dave! That's why I didn't come looking for you! I thought *you* would kill *me* after I got saved!"

Snake and I laughed and cried and praised the Lord together. "Dave, did you know I've been ordained to the ministry?"

"You are? I've been licensed! Hasn't God been good to us?"

After reminiscing a little more, we agreed

wholeheartedly that life in Jesus is the greatest. As far as we knew, all of our former "friends" were either dead or in prison. For both of us, our meeting together was a fitting climax to our salvation, the frosting on the cake! The tears were quite appropriate.

Chapter 12

New Frontiers

God was teaching me new things almost daily. Being Production Manager for an exploding nationwide ministry continued to stretch my abilities. Then came the event that taught me a whole new way of doing business for the Lord.

Jim Bakker decided the PTL Club should carry the JESUS '77 rally near Mount Union, Pennsylvania. Tens of thousands of young people (and adults, too) poured into Agape Camp Farm. As Production Manager, I had the job of organizing the entire television operation. The job was over my head; indeed, several of the PTL Club executives frankly expected me to make a mess of it. I knew I needed the wisdom of God. I had to transport, store, protect, assemble and dismantle a million dollars worth of equipment. My crew totalled fifty, with dozens of support people remaining in Charlotte. I had to provide housing, three meals each day, and, I discovered, even a couple of disciplinary actions for my crew. Everything had to go right: Jim Bakker demands excellence.

The job seemed impossible, so I spent a lot of time in prayer about it. Reminding me of important matters I had overlooked, God showed me how to produce the whole event. After we arrived at JESUS '77, I sensed in my spirit the assurance of being led by the Spirit of God through every step. On a number of occasions, the Holy Spirit told me to do things that seemed wrong, or at least, unnecessary. Later, these actions proved important in every case. The entire operation was a great success. But God taught me something that today is of immense value — how to hear His voice in business decisions. *That* was the greatest lesson of JESUS '77!

The PTL Club had just purchased a television station — Channel 17 — in Canton, Ohio. Very quickly the station developed problems — serious problems. Jim Bakker wanted to send someone they could trust to Canton quickly, and he knew I was the one. So I became Manager of Channel 17, PTL's Christian television station in Canton, Ohio, in the fall of 1977.

It was a most difficult situation. In addition to the serious financial condition of the station, I discovered that promises had been made to the

Christians in eastern Ohio — promises that were not being kept. I did my best to help the situation in Canton. God enabled me to get the finances straightened out, and I tried to fulfill as much as was in my power to accomplish. By the grace of God, I survived fifteen months of difficult problems in Canton.

One day I was driving along a busy highway near Canton — the weather was bitterly cold — when I saw a little white poodle in the middle of the road. Because of my love for suffering animals, I just had to stop. Braving the heavy traffic, I hurried to rescue the dog. His legs appeared to be frozen, and he was crying bitterly. After very nearly being hit by several cars, I made my way to the dog, but he ran away from me. Again and again I almost caught that half-frozen little poodle, but each time he escaped my grasp. I finally had to give up because of the danger from the speeding traffic.

Almost in tears, I reluctantly crawled back into the warm car, when the Holy Spirit spoke gently in my heart: "That's the way *you* were through all those years. The more I tried to save you from danger, the more you ran from me." Then I *really* felt like crying. The next few miles were filled with my sincerest praises to the Lord Jesus, who had pursued me so lovingly through all my misery, until I finally let Him take me into His care.

One unexpected blessing occurred in Canton. I didn't realize what had happened to our marriage while I was Production Manager in Charlotte. So in love with my work that I rarely saw Brinda for any length of time, we had slowly drifted apart. In Canton the severe winter weather forced us together again, and God used those hours to restore our marriage.

The entire Northeast suffered under two severe winters while we were in Canton. I promised myself that if God would just get me out of there, I'd stay in the South the rest of my life.

In early 1979 I was appointed Director of Television Operations back in warm Charlotte. Suddenly I was responsible for one hundred thirty employees! It could have been frightening, but by now God had taught me the secret of listening for the voice of His Spirit in business decisions. Besides, the promotion got me out of the cold northern weather.

Having formerly been Production Manager of PTL, I knew many of the problems. We were doing twenty-five television productions every week, and there was no time or space for any more. But the Lord showed me how to institute a scheduling system, under which we were able to do one hundred productions every week! All in the same limited facilities! I started cross-training employees, too. We'd put a cameraman in engineering for a period, or an engineer in scheduling. It was almost comical to see how each employee began understanding the other guy's problems.

When we were in Canton, I had asked Brinda to become my secretary and administrative assistant. She was allowed to continue in this capacity in Charlotte, and we found that we enjoyed working together. Indeed, I soon discovered that I could hardly function effectively without Brinda at my right hand. The little waitress had become a highly skilled administrative assistant!

We had technical problems, too. Affiliate stations had been complaining ever since the beginning of the PTL Club about the poor quality of our videotapes. To the trained eye of an engineer, the complaints were justified. Then God gave us Jerry Foreman, an excellent Director of Engineering, and one of the best in the nation. Our engineering standards were so poor that Jerry went right back home to Ohio the day after he was hired. But the Lord spoke to him, telling him that he had been *called* to the PTL Club, so Jerry obediently returned to Charlotte.

I certainly sympathized with Jerry, so he and I instituted a quality control program that quickly changed the PTL Club "picture quality" from pitiful to excellent. Soon Scientific Atlanta was stating publicly that the PTL Club had the best TV picture in the nation. *Broadcast Management & Engineering* did a cover story on the PTL Club's startling transformation. Jerry Foreman and I were very proud, but we both knew that God had shown us how to accomplish that goal. The two of us developed a wonderful relationship of mutual respect.

One day I was told I'd be supervising a new department, Research and Development, with instructions to investigate areas of possible improvement for all of PTL. I began learning how business plans for the future. Over the years I had worked at every major job at the PTL Club except accounting. God had rather quickly trained me in nearly all areas of expertise for leading a Christian television ministry. The work was so satisfying! To add to my enjoyment, the Executive Vice President told me I was in line for another promotion; he even described my future duties. Looking forward to another new challenge, I came home one evening to find Brinda sobbing.

"What's happened? Why are you crying?"

"I don't understand it, David. God spoke to

me this evening, and He said that we can't work at PTL any longer. He's moving us."

"Well, if God wants us to leave here, He can speak to me!" I didn't want to talk about leaving: I was part of a ministry with a vision for the world! So I just put it out of my mind.

Some days later Brinda brought up the subject again: "Honey, the Lord says we're going to work for a smaller ministry somewhere up North."

"Forget it!" I blurted out. "I've had all I can take of snow and ice in Canton!"

"David," Brinda said gently after a few more days, "the Lord says we can't stay here." Her little quotations from the Lord were unsettling.

One evening the telephone rang. It was Russ Bixler, President of WPCB-TV, Channel 40, in Pittsburgh. "David, would you please pray about coming here as our General Manager?"

I didn't dare listen for a voice in my spirit; I was afraid of what He might say. But Brinda smiled knowingly. I tried to talk as calmly as I could. Why should I get unnerved? After all, this is only the *tenth* job offer I've received from other Christian TV ministries this year! I'm right where I belong! "I really appreciate your offer, Russ, but I'm quite satisfied here. God has lots of work for me here."

We talked further, but that still, small voice refused to be squelched. The Lord spoke softly, "If he asks you to come for a visit, accept the invitation!"

An instant later Russ said boldly, "David, I think you should come to Pittsburgh for a visit!"

"Okay!" The word burst out of my mouth before I even thought of it. Russ was startled that I had agreed within a split second. In fact, I was startled myself! Thinking more about it, I began hedging: "I know you need help, Russ. I think I can give you some counsel. And I know lots of good people too; perhaps I can help you find a General Manager."

Russ and I agreed upon a date, and I arrived in Pittsburgh to discover that he had scheduled a meeting of his Board of Directors. Each of them asked me a lot of questions, then they all looked at each other as if I was to be their next General Manager. "Wait a minute!" I protested. "I only came to offer some counsel for your problems!" They appreciated the advice, but they didn't want to hear my other suggestions for the position of General Manager!

The snow was coming down heavily in Pittsburgh as the temperature was dropping rapidly. Outside the wet mud was freezing, and snow was piling up on top of the ice. After loaning me a company car, Russ said he'd lead me to the motel in his car. But, while going down the hill, Russ slid into the ditch beside the icy road and, rather than hit his car, I piled into the ditch right behind him! Both cars were stuck in the snow. It was one of the worst winter days they had had in Pittsburgh! We slogged through the blowing snow to get a ride with someone else. "God," I murmured, "just get me back to Charlotte, and I'll never come North again!"

Russ insisted that I call Brinda. I told her on the telephone I didn't want to come to Pittsburgh. "What do *you* think?" I asked, after assuming she was already programed for the correct answer.

"Well, I'm packing!" Brinda responded quickly. And she was!

"What did she say?" Russ queried.

"She said she's packing."

Russ laughed, but I felt trapped. "I guess we'll come to Pittsburgh," I added softly.

On the plane back to Charlotte, I thought, "What's the matter with me? I can't go to Pittsburgh! That just doesn't make any sense! Why should I leave an international ministry for a single market? I'm not going to let my emotions overrule my good judgment." And I resolved to call Russ Bixler to tell him that I would *not* be coming to Pittsburgh.

Brinda didn't argue. She merely pleaded with me to pray some more. She knew what God had told her.

Some days later I was driving alone in Charlotte, praising the Lord, when suddenly the air in the car seemed to grow heavy, almost suffocating. The hair on my arms stood up as if charged with electricity. I knew the Presence of God was with me. It was awesome! His voice spoke quietly, "This is my will concerning you!"

I knew exactly what the Lord meant by that statement. I parked the car at the first telephone booth and called Russ, telling him that I'd be coming. He was a little surprised by my call. Everyone in Pittsburgh knew I was coming; why was this call necessary? Then I called Brinda, and she was delighted that I'd finally heard from the Lord.

Resigning from PTL was extremely difficult for both of us. Some said they knew that God wanted us in Pittsburgh; others suggested angrily that God would punish us if we left PTL.

One major job remained before leaving. The PTL Club would be erecting and operating a display booth at the annual National Religious

Broadcasters' Convention.   It was January 1981, and I had already been assigned to supervise that job in Washington, D.C.   I agreed to resign from the PTL Television Network *after* the convention.

Brinda and I were living in a mobile home, and we had some personal belongings stored elsewhere.   So I decided to drive our little car to Pittsburgh with the excess articles, store it at Channel 40, and fly on to Washington.   Then, after the convention, I'd pull the mobile home to Pittsburgh with our pick-up truck.   I am not a person who sheds tears, except under extreme circumstances, yet I cried all the way to Pittsburgh. I didn't want to leave PTL!   By the time I arrived at the Greater Pittsburgh Airport, I was quite depressed.   "Lord," I begged, "please do something to comfort me!"

"David Kelton!"   I looked around to see John Gimenez, Pastor of Rock Church in Virginia Beach.   To our delight we were to be on the same flight — even assigned adjacent seats.   John ministered to me so wonderfully as we shared the ride to Washington.   By the time we landed, I was rejoicing about moving to Pittsburgh.

God went to great lengths to provide John Gimenez for me: John was flying from the West Coast to Norfolk on an earlier flight, and had merely stepped off his plane in Pittsburgh to make a telephone call, and the plane had taken off without him. He was without his coat, briefcase and baggage. It almost ruined his day. With a smile, I told John I thought the Lord had given me very personal attention, but John wasn't nearly as happy about it as I was.

Brinda and I went through a real struggle to get to Pittsburgh. Everything seemed to go wrong! I got food poisoning from a restaurant meal and Brinda developed the worst case of the flu she ever had. And, just as I expected, Pittsburgh was covered with ice and snow. Brinda was extremely sick when we arrived. I went to work on Monday morning, leaving Brinda alone in the trailer. Within hours several employees of Channel 40 were in the trailer, praying for her. The fever broke, and she slept until the next morning, when she got dressed and went to work with me. Thus we were introduced to a ministry where everybody believes in miracles.

Chapter 13

Learning to Expect the Impossible

They had to believe in miracles in Pittsburgh! Channel 40 was in such a mess that only some miracles could pull them out — the station was nearly bankrupt. Before I left Charlotte, I figured that God would have me stay a year or so, get the station straightened out, and then move to another TV ministry that needed help. But TV40's problems were immense, and they were strange: a perfectly-good computer was giving out information that didn't make sense; a mud slide was corroding the bottom guy-wire holding the 842-foot tower; four klystron tubes had blown mysteriously in a brief time (the tubes cost more than $30,000 each). These weren't ordinary problems: they seemed diabolically conceived. I knew I'd really need to hear from God.

All my various transfers and promotions within PTL had served a purpose for my work at Channel 40, having given me a well-rounded

education in Christian television.   Working
closely with Russ Bixler and Oleen Eagle, Vice
President of the station, and with the auditors,
who were also Christians, we began to make
changes.   Each change came after prayer, with
Russ and Oleen supporting me.   Improvements
came steadily.

Financially, though, Channel 40 still
languished, deeply in debt.   Six months after I
arrived, God spoke to Russ Bixler, saying that we
were all suffering from a "spirit of poverty."   The
Lord told him we were blaming the weak economy
for our shortages.   God said that if we would stop
looking to the area's financial condition and seek
only Him, He would provide.   Russ called an
immediate meeting of the full staff, issuing orders
that no one should ever again use the economy as
an excuse for our poor financial condition.   So
we began to praise the Lord for all the station's
needs.   Within three months we received a
"miracle gift" of $100,000!   Within six more
months, Channel 40 was current on its bills — for
the first time ever!

I noticed that a number of my former
employees at PTL were calling me, even visiting
me in Pittsburgh.   One by one they would tell me
that God was moving them to Pittsburgh — and I
hadn't solicited any of those calls.   Each one who
came was an answer to prayer.   When the

engineering department needed strengthening, Jerry Foreman came from PTL for a visit, and the Lord spoke to him about working at Channel 40 as he was driving up the hill to the station. I could hardly believe that God would give us one of the best chief engineers in the nation!

So many former PTL employees came to work for Channel 40 that the executives in Charlotte began calling me "The Pittsburgh Pirate"!

One day, shortly after arriving in Pittsburgh, I was walking toward Russ's office, when my left knee buckled, as it had done occasionally throughout the years. The pain was excruciating, as usual. Russ saw my face, and asked what was wrong. Within a second he had his hand on my left knee, praying. The knee has never collapsed since that day, the pain is completely gone, and I can walk up stairs normally after years of taking one step at a time. The only remaining physical problem from the years of abusing my body is the occasional swelling and pain in my left ankle.

Russ Bixler and Oleen Eagle have been a joy to work with. We rarely have a serious disagreement. Channel 40's ministry is characterized by honesty, openness and love; I noticed immediately that there is no manipulation of people at TV40. Russ is different from most other Christian television leaders: he doesn't pretend to be a skilled businessman and executive. Recognizing his limitations as an administrator, Russ emphasizes his calling to be a *spiritual* leader. He provides Oleen and me with a climate in which our God-given managerial talents may be expressed. The Lord has put together the most wonderful staff of dedicated people at TV40!

We were all so delighted once when a large company was negotiating with me concerning a rental of some of our facilities. TV40 rarely becomes involved in such business matters because of its nonprofit status. This time, however, their rental of our property was essential. The company offered me a certain amount of money, which they insisted was fair. As I prayed, God showed me how much they should pay. The figure was quite high — far above what this large company was offering.

Four executives cornered me at a lunch meeting. They were rather intimidating. Suggesting that TV40 was too small to be dictating terms, they looked to me, expecting my meek agreement. The Lord gave me such boldness that I said, "But God is bigger than your whole company! And if He wants you to pay this price, then that's what you're going to pay!"

They were astonished! Returning crestfallen to their offices, they had to get higher authority to negotiate further. I refused to budge; I knew what God had told me. Returning again and again with ever-higher offers, the company finally agreed to the Lord's exact price. I even told them we wanted the cash up front — and we got it!

God gave that miracle in the nick of time. I had their check in my hands, and we were moving into our newly completed, larger studio in two days. Needing two more cameras for the bigger studio quickly, we heard about two almost-new cameras for sale in Washington, D.C. I drove to Washington to find myself dealing with a very difficult businessman. He had already suffered losses from two large Christian ministries, so he didn't even want to do business with me. Again God gave me a boldness. When you know the mind of God in a business matter, confidence and certainty follow. I came home with the two cameras — and lots more valuable equipment which the businessman added freely. When TV40's engineers saw everything, they were like children under a Christmas tree. All of it was purchased as the result of the check from that one large corporation!

Jerry Foreman and I instituted a quality control program at Channel 40 — similar to what we had done in Charlotte. Today TV40 broadcasts the best picture of all the UHF stations in western Pennsylvania, and we're closing rapidly on the quality of the VHF stations.

Gradually, the Lord was straightening out the situation at TV40. Thinking that it might soon be time for us to move on to another Christian ministry, Brinda and I continued to live in our mobile home. We felt we should be free to leave when God called. I mentioned this to Oleen one day, and her response really shook me.

"Did God speak to you, telling you to come to Pittsburgh?" she asked.

"Yes, very clearly."

"Then," she added, "He'll speak to you in the same way when it's time to leave!"

Since that day I've been wondering if He'll *ever* tell us to leave. I truly love all of TV40's employees and volunteers! All through the twenty years I lived in Charlotte, I never quite felt at home. If someone would ask me where I was from, my response was usually "Kansas City." We've lived in Pennsylvania less than three years, and already I've heard myself tell people that I'm from Pittsburgh. I really feel at home here!

Demos Shakarian came to Pittsburgh a couple of years ago to meet with the Full Gospel

Businessmen's local officers. About fifty area chapters were represented at the meeting. Demos requested that I give a brief report of my leg healing there. As a result, I have received many dozens of invitations to speak at FGBMFI banquets, so many that I only occasionally have an open weekend.

God really uses that testimony. Having shared it literally hundreds of times, I can say truthfully that there is always someone who accepts Jesus as Lord, and sometimes a surprising number of people respond. Some of those who have accepted Jesus Christ after hearing me have done so at the last moment — just before a planned suicide, for example. It's God's testimony, and He knows how to use it best.

An organization known as The Committee for International Goodwill celebrates a "Man of the Year" banquet annually. Demos Shakarian was honored as the 1982 recipient at the award dinner held in Anaheim, California. To my great surprise, Demos paid my way to fly to the banquet, where I told how God had lengthened my leg so spectacularly in response to Demos's prayer.

Pat Robertson, an earlier recipient of the award, was present at the "Man of the Year" banquet, and he invited me to share my story on the 700 Club. I do not enjoy being on television — my ministry is behind the camera — so I was terribly nervous on the 700 Club. Yet, the studio audience laughed and praised God through the entire testimony!

One evening I was sharing my story at a Full Gospel Businessmen's banquet near Pittsburgh. One of our employees had asked her parents to attend. We visited their home following the meeting, where her skeptical father said, "You don't expect me to believe that story, do you?"

"Naw!" I taunted him. "I made it up just for you!"

"Well, I don't believe it!"

"You think you have trouble believing it? How do you think I felt when a 'dead' Man healed my leg?" Our employee's father is still pondering that question.

Mom Kelton, as she is affectionately known — my Mom — who prayed so faithfully all those years, today has a most unusual ministry of her own. Kids, such as I was, will sit at her feet, many of them being delivered from crime, drugs, alcohol and illicit sex. Mom doesn't condemn — she just loves and teaches about Jesus. Churches will fly her many miles just so she can share what she knows about God.

When Tim received a call to supervise a

mission area in Papua, New Guinea, Mom immediately made plans to visit him as soon as possible. She ministered in Papuan churches and mission stations for six months, thus fulfilling, at least partially, her childhood vision to be a foreign missionary. Before she left for New Guinea, Mom told me privately, "If I die there, don't bring my body back to America. I'd be thrilled to die on the mission field!"

Mom fell into a mysterious coma while preaching in one of those mission churches. Tim called from New Guinea, telling us to pray. We were wondering, "Did Mom know she would die there?"

As we were praying for her at TV40, God spoke to Russ Bixler: "Everything is going to be all right!" That comforted me a bit, but we didn't know if the prophecy meant He would heal Mom, or take her to heaven with Him! I knew she'd be happy either way. But God healed her, and she still ministers across the eastern United States.

Very frankly, as I said at the beginning, I'm embarrassed to tell this very personal story. Now you understand my reluctance. I've been so ashamed of myself, yet I know I'm forgiven — forgiven by God of *all* my sin!

You can be forgiven too! And *you* can receive God's free gift of eternal life, just as I have!

Just pray this prayer out loud — and mean it!

Jesus, I confess that I am a sinner. Forgive my sins, and wash me in Your precious blood. Come into my heart. I understand as I repent of my sins that I will not commit those sins anymore.

I confess that You are *my* Lord, *my* Savior, and that you have granted me eternal life. I now believe that You have cleansed me of all sin, according to the Scripture.

I thank you for accepting me just as I am, and for writing my name in Your Book of Life. Amen.

Epilogue

The Healings Continue

Russ Bixler and I took a week off to begin writing this book. Traveling to North Carolina's Outer Banks, a beautiful, windswept strip of land, we spent many hours there discussing my story. I was quite uncomfortable, but Russ insisted that I tell it all.

We prayed together, asking the Lord to enable me to recall all the important events. Because I had been stoned on drugs or alcohol so much of my life, I had to depend upon others' memories for much of the testimony. Yet I was astonished at the many experiences God brought to my conscious mind during that week. "Do we have to tell *that*?" was my repeated protest. It was not a happy week for me.

Yet, each time I'd describe an event to Russ, I'd seem to feel better once it was out in the open. God was granting me a blessed therapy, an inner healing of terrible memories.

"Uh-oh!" I said one day, as I was describing some of my sordid past.

"What's the matter?" asked Russ.

"I've got to take Brinda out to dinner after we get home. I thought I'd confessed all my lies to her, but that's one I forgot."

Russ asked about everything — names, dates, places, sequences of events. Oh, how I hated to tell him about walking out on Judy and my little Cindy! But Russ persisted. Suddenly he looked up at me and exclaimed, "David! Cindy is not your child!"

"Why do you say that?"

"Look at the months involved!" Russ went over the dates in detail.

I didn't believe him. I went to the telephone in our motel and called Mom. She exploded! "Of course Cindy wasn't your baby!" Then she gave me more exact dates, all of which made it quite clear. "You were so stoned all the time, you wouldn't listen to me. I tried to tell you!"

I was free! Free at last from the remaining guilt that I hadn't allowed God's grace to cover!

I was so relieved and so much at peace that I said we should celebrate. "Let's go fishing!"

Russ called the president of the local Full Gospel Businessmen's chapter, and Bill Tolson graciously took us surf-fishing for bluefish. It was great! But those "blues" have such sharp teeth that they chewed off my lines. I had to walk several hundred yards in deep sand to purchase more lures.

I had walked only a short distance when I remembered that my left ankle was not strong enough to walk in the soft sand. Yet, it wasn't swollen, and it wasn't hurting, so I continued walking. On the way back, each step became a moment of greater praise. By the time I arrived back with Russ and Bill, I knew the ankle was healed — totally, every whit whole, the final touch by my loving Father in heaven! I am completely healed, and He did it all!

I'm still astonished when I think of all that God has done for me — and I'm filled with anticipation about things yet to come.

Why? — I wonder sometimes — Why did God single out David Kelton to declare, "Chosen to Live!"?

"God chose the foolish things of the world to shame the wise; God chose the weak things of the world to shame the strong."

1 Cor. 1:27 (NIV)